Oxford School *Shakespeare*

JULIUS CAESAR

edited by
Roma Gill, OBE
M.A. *Cantab.*, B. Litt. *Oxon*

OXFORD
UNIVERSITY PRESS

OXFORD

UNIVERSITY PRESS

Great Clarendon Street, Oxford OX2 6DP

Oxford University Press is a department of the University of Oxford.
It furthers the University's objective of excellence in research, scholarship, and
education by publishing worldwide in

Oxford New York

Auckland Bangkok Buenos Aires Cape Town Chennai Dar es Salaam Delhi
Hong Kong Istanbul Karachi Kolkata Kuala Lumpur Madrid Melbourne
Mexico City Mumbai Nairobi São Paulo Shanghai Taipei Tokyo Toronto

Oxford is a registered trade mark of Oxford University Press
in the UK and in certain other countries

Trade edition first published 1994
Reprinted in this new edition 2001

ISBN 0 19 832027 2

5 7 9 10 8 6

Illustrations by Alexy Pendle

All photographs by Donald Cooper/Photostage, except p. 124. Cover shows
Julian Glover as Cassius and John Nettles as Brutus in the Royal Shakespeare
Company's 1995 production of *Julius Caesar*.

For Richard

Oxford School Shakespeare
edited by Roma Gill

A Midsummer Night's Dream	Hamlet
Romeo and Juliet	King Lear
As You Like It	Henry V
Macbeth	The Winter's Tale
Julius Caesar	Antony and Cleopatra
The Merchant of Venice	The Tempest
Henry IV Part I	Richard II
Twelfth Night	Coriolanus
The Taming of the Shrew	Measure for Measure
Othello	Much Ado About Nothing
Love's Labour's Lost	

Typeset by Herb Bowes Graphics, Oxford
Printed and bound by Creative Print and Design Wales, Ebbw Vale

Contents

Introduction

About the Play

Julius Caesar—the Man and the Play

What do you know about Julius Caesar? In Shakespeare's play Mark Antony, Caesar's best friend, calls him 'the noblest man That ever lived in the tide of times' (3, 1, 256–7); and Brutus, one of the men who murdered him, acknowledges that he has killed 'the foremost man of all this world' (4, 3, 22). What did Caesar do to deserve such high praise?

Shakespeare isn't going to show us. The character who gives the play its title appears in only three scenes, and speaks very few lines—none of them particularly memorable. On his first appearance, in public, he gives orders ('When Caesar says "Do this", it is performed'—1, 2, 10); but at home with his wife Calpurnia (*Act 2*, Scene 2) he seems less resolute—willing to listen to superstitions and yield to persuasions. He is last seen alive in the Capitol, where he refuses to repeal a sentence of banishment and, unawares, gives the cue for the conspirators' action. They stab—and Caesar dies. Not a very impressive performance!

But Julius Caesar was part of the national curriculum in the Elizabethan education system. Latin was the most important subject in every grammar school, and pupils studied the history as well as the language and literature of Rome. Shakespeare's first audiences (unless they had been asleep in the classroom) would have brought their general knowledge to the playhouse, and would not have needed biographical details to justify the claims of Antony and Brutus.

Early in the first century BC three men—Pompey, Crassus, and Julius Caesar—united to form a triumvirate (from the Latin *tres viri* = three men) to govern Rome and its provinces. In 53 BC Crassus was killed whilst fighting the Parthians; neither Pompey nor Caesar could agree to share power with the other, and civil war broke out. At the battle of Pharsalia (48 BC) Caesar defeated Pompey; then, a little later, he conquered Pompey's two sons at the battle of Munda. The play opens with Caesar's return from this last victory.

Caesar now appeared to have absolute power; but the name of 'king' was hated and feared in Rome. Although the people loved him, some of the senators and aristocrats were afraid that he would become a tyrant—and the chief among these were Marcus Brutus and Cassius. In the civil war they had both fought on Pompey's side against Caesar, but Caesar had pardoned and befriended Brutus and, at Brutus's request, recalled Cassius to Rome. Despite this clemency, they conspired to assassinate him in 42 BC.

Julius Caesar was born in 100 BC, and before he was twenty years old he had become a distinguished soldier. In the course of a glittering military and political career, he fought and held office in Africa, Spain, and France, and he extended the Roman rule to the Atlantic and to the English Channel. In the intervals between military campaigns he devoted himself, with amazing energy, to re-establishing order in Rome, improving the economic situation, regulating taxation, codifying the law, and instituting a public library. Caesar was also a gifted writer: his *Commentaries* on the Gallic Wars and on the Civil War are masterpieces of narrative skill, and although other writings have not survived, we know that they included a textbook of grammar (written during a journey across the Alps), and a treatise on the stars. He was an expert astronomer and mathematician, and the calendar that he devised in 46 BC is the one we use today, honouring his name in the month of Julius—July.

In the play Caesar is murdered at the beginning of *Act 3*, and you may first think it odd that the hero should vanish from the stage before the play is half-finished. But although the man is dead, his spirit lives on. It is present in the minds of those who murdered him, and of those who seek to avenge the murder. We are so conscious of this unseen presence that it is no surprise when the spirit materializes, and the ghost of Caesar appears to Brutus before the battle at Philippi. Brutus, too, is unperturbed, and accepts with equanimity the promise of another encounter—'Why, I will see thee at Philippi then' (4, 3, 286).

The tragedy of *Julius Caesar* is not the tragedy of one man alone. Brutus shares the tragic fate—and so too does Cassius, although to a lesser extent. The tragedy was not completed when Caesar died in the Capitol, and Brutus makes this plain when he talks to Cassius before Philippi:

> this same day
> Must end that work the Ides of March begun.

(5, 1, 112–13)

Although the conspirators were defeated, full democracy never returned to Rome. A second triumvirate was formed, consisting of Antony, Lepidus, and Octavius, but Lepidus was the weak link (as Antony remarks in 4, 1, 12–40); and Antony himself was well known to be 'a masker and a reveller' (5, 1, 62). Only Octavius, called 'a peevish schoolboy' by Cassius (5, 1, 61) because he was only eighteen at the time of the murder, was able to sustain his role as one of the rulers of the great Roman empire. He was Julius Caesar's great-nephew and heir, and he later adopted the name 'Caesar', with the addition 'Augustus'—titles which were ever afterwards bestowed on rulers of the Roman empire. In 27 BC Octavius took the further title of 'Princeps'—the chief one—and Rome ceased to be a republic.

Shakespeare had no doubt about the eternal relevance of his theme, and it is tempting to think that the words of Cassius might be the dramatist's prophetic judgement on his own play:

> How many ages hence
> Shall this our lofty scene be acted over
> In states unborn and accents yet unknown!
>
> (3, 1, 111–13)

But Shakespeare seems to have taken very little thought about the future of his dramatic writings: the manuscripts were no longer his property after they were bought by the dramatic company, and *Julius Caesar*, like many more of his plays, was not published during Shakespeare's lifetime.

Leading Characters in the Play

Julius Caesar The greatest and most powerful of the Romans, and the last of the three men who formed the first triumvirate. He has always been ambitious—and it is now suspected that he wants to be king, and sole ruler of the Roman Empire.

Octavius Caesar The great-nephew of Julius Caesar, and heir to his uncle's wealth and position. Only eighteen at the time of Caesar's assassination, he joins Mark Antony in making war on the conspirators.

Mark Antony Caesar's loyal friend, who stirs up the opposition when Caesar is murdered, and, with Octavius Caesar and Lepidus, leads the attack on the conspirators.

Marcus Brutus Caesar's great friend, who joins in the conspiracy because his love for Rome is even greater than his love for his friend. An idealist, he assumes that others will share his high principles.

Caius Cassius The instigator and organizer of the conspiracy against Julius Caesar. He is a fanatic, but he is also a practical man who knows his own limitations and those of other men. Although not a very attractive character at first, he becomes more noble—even heroic—in defeat.

Calpurnia The wife of Julius Caesar, whose prophetic dream foretells the assassination.

Portia The wife of Marcus Brutus, who is devoted to her husband and distressed by his anxieties. Through her we see another aspect of Brutus—the gentle, loving husband.

Synopsis

ACT 1

Scene 1 The tribunes are angry because some tradesmen are taking a holiday to celebrate Julius Caesar's triumphant entry into Rome.

Scene 2 Caesar, going to see the Lupercal games, is warned to beware the Ides of March. Brutus and Cassius discuss Caesar's career, and Cassius warns of potential danger. Caesar's procession returns, and Casca describes how Caesar refused to accept a crown; Cassius and Brutus arrange another meeting.

Scene 3 A terrible storm is raging; Casca tells Cicero about some unnatural sights, but Cicero is unimpressed. Cassius, rejoicing in the weather and the omens, tells Casca of the conspiracy and of his hopes that Brutus will also join the rebels.

ACT 2

Scene 1 Brutus finds a letter urging him to action. Cassius introduces other conspirators, and they plan the assassination of Caesar. Brutus's wife, Portia, is worried about him, but another visitor, Ligarius, adds his support to the conspiracy.

Scene 2 Caesar has also been disturbed by a stormy night; his wife tries to persuade him not to go to the Capitol because the omens are unfavourable, but Decius Brutus is scornful, and Caesar sets out for the Capitol, accompanied by the conspirators.

Scene 3 Artemidorus reads the letter he will give to Caesar.

Scene 4 Portia is anxious to know what is happening in the Capitol, and the words of a soothsayer give her more cause for alarm.

ACT 3

Scene 1   Caesar, ignoring Artemidorus and the soothsayer, takes his seat in the Senate House. He refuses to grant a petition—and gives the conspirators their cue to stab him. Brutus takes control, and Antony asks to be allowed to speak at Caesar's funeral. When he is alone on stage, Antony prophesies civil war—and sends a message to Octavius.

Scene 2   Brutus reasons with the citizens, and convinces them that Caesar was a potential tyrant—then Antony makes his funeral oration, speaking of Caesar's love for Rome and its citizens, showing them Caesar's body, and reading his will. The citizens are roused to mutiny, and threaten to murder the conspirators. Antony learns that Octavius has entered the city—and that Brutus and Cassius have fled.

Scene 3   Cinna the poet meets an angry mob: they question him briefly—then kill him.

ACT 4

Scene 1   Antony, Octavius, and Lepidus plan their strategy.

Scene 2   Brutus and Cassius are beginning to quarrel.

Scene 3   The quarrel continues; a poet tries to make peace, but Brutus dismisses him—and then explains to Cassius that he is distressed because Portia is dead. The rebel armies must now move on to Philippi to meet Antony and the Roman forces, but first Brutus needs to sleep. The ghost of Caesar appears.

ACT 5

Scene 1   Antony and Octavius confront the rebels, then withdraw to prepare for battle. Cassius tells Messala about the omens he has witnessed; he is resolved to die rather than be captured by Antony, and says his formal farewell to Brutus.

Scene 2   Battle has commenced—and Brutus is hopeful.

Scene 3   Deserted by his soldiers, Cassius orders his slave to kill him. His best friend, Titinius, bringing news of victory, finds the body—and kills himself. Brutus continues the fight.

Scene 4   Lucilius, pretending to be Brutus, is captured by Antony's soldiers, but Antony recognizes him.

Scene 5   The rebels are defeated, Brutus kills himself, and Antony speaks his obituary.

Julius Caesar: commentary

ACT 1

Scene 1   Flavius and Murellus are annoyed when they find that the Roman citizens have taken a holiday from work and are crowding on to the streets 'to see Caesar, and to rejoice in his triumph'. A cobbler tries to joke with the tribunes, but they are too angry to laugh. Murellus reproaches the people for their disloyalty: they have forgotten their love for Pompey, and now Caesar is their hero. The blank verse and dignified language of the tribune's speech contrasts with the cobbler's colloquial prose, and mark a kind of class distinction between the major characters in the play (who are identified by name), and the ordinary citizens, the men-in-the-street.

When they hear what Murellus has to say, the people are silent and slink away from the scene. Flavius explains what is happening:

> See where their basest mettle be not mov'd:
> They vanish tongue-tied in their guiltiness.

The Roman citizens are very important in *Julius Caesar*, and provide an essential background to the action. They are influenced by emotion, not by reason, and their affections are not to be trusted: in the past they cheered for Pompey; now they are welcoming Caesar, the man who has defeated Pompey; and soon we shall hear them applauding the men who have murdered Caesar.

Flavius and Murellus are determined to insult Caesar by tearing down the decorations intended to honour him. Their conversation gives us a hint of what is to come—we shall hear from other characters who also fear that Caesar will 'soar above the view of men | And keep us all in servile fearfulness'.

Scene 2   As the tribunes depart, Caesar's ceremonial procession enters, and we have a brief glimpse of the great man. The ominous words 'Beware the ides of March' are spoken, and then the procession leaves the stage. Brutus and Cassius stay behind. Very gently, Cassius tries to win Brutus's confidence. He flatters Brutus a little, then declares his own honesty. An offstage shout from the crowds attending Caesar startles Brutus, and he accidentally speaks his thoughts aloud: 'I do fear the people | Choose Caesar for their king'. The word 'fear' encourages

Cassius to proceed with an attack on Caesar. He recalls two instances when Caesar showed weakness, but Cassius speaks as though the weakness were moral, and not merely physical. Cassius shows a mean spirit here, but Brutus does not seem to notice—or perhaps his attention is distracted by another shout from the crowd. Cassius returns to flattery, reminding Brutus of his own reputation and that of his ancestor, the Brutus who expelled Tarquin from Rome. At last Brutus promises that he will give some thought to the matters that Cassius has raised.

Some relaxation of tension is needed now, and it is supplied by Casca's account of the ceremony with the crown—'yet 'twas not a crown neither, 'twas one of these coronets'. Again there is a contrast between prose and verse, and between the colloquial, idiomatic language of Casca's speeches and the formal, dignified utterances of Brutus and Cassius.

When Cassius is alone, he points out how easily Brutus's nobility of character can be perverted; we realize, too, what a dangerous man Cassius is, and the threat to Caesar becomes very frightening:

> let Caesar seat him sure,
> For we will shake him, or worse days endure.

The threat is echoed in the thunder that heralds the next scene.

Scene 3   The storm renews the tension. Both the Romans and the Elizabethans believed that the world of Nature (the macrocosm) and the political world of human affairs (the microcosm) reflected each other, and that disturbances in one foretold, or paralleled, unusual events in the other. Of course, there were sceptics in both nations who denied that there was any link between the two worlds: Cicero is such a sceptic, but Casca is convinced that the storm is intended as a warning from the gods. Cassius, however, welcomes the storm, and shows his fanaticism as he walks unprotected. He interprets the night's unnatural events as being parallels to the monstrosity in the Roman world, and Casca understands: "Tis Caesar that you mean, is it not, Cassius?'

Cassius tests Casca's feelings about Caesar, then invites him to take part in the conspiracy. When Cinna joins them, we learn that the plot is well advanced.

ACT 2

Scene 1   We now recognize that the play is operating on two time-scales. Cicero's opening remark in *Act 1*, Scene 3 ('Good even, Casca, brought you Caesar home?') suggests that Casca has just left Caesar, having escorted him home after the celebrations of the Lupercal (*Act 1*, Scene 2). When this scene ends, Cassius observes that 'it is after midnight'. The conspirators go in search of Brutus and find him at home, just as dawn is breaking ('yon grey lines | That fret the clouds are messengers of day'). But more than *hours* have elapsed. The storm gives an impression of continuity between *Act 1*, Scene 3 and *Act 2*, Scene 1; but we have in fact moved from 15 February (the feast of Lupercal) to 15 (the ides) March. Brutus has had weeks, not hours, in which to decide upon a course of action, and his soliloquy now reflects the thoughts of that whole period.

A soliloquy—words, not intended for a listener, spoken by a character when he is thinking aloud—is, by the conventions of Elizabethan drama, always to be trusted. Brutus now states his dilemma clearly: he has no personal grudge against Caesar, and no reason to distrust him—but, on the other hand, all power corrupts, and if Caesar is given imperial power, he may prove a danger to Rome. His honour and his patriotism urge Brutus to take action against Caesar, and although he recognizes the ugliness of the situation, he steps forward to welcome the conspirators. He shakes each one by the hand, speaking his name in token of fellowship (and incidentally introducing the different characters to the audience).

Brutus shows his idealism when he rejects the suggestion that they should swear an oath of allegiance. He has taken command of the situation now, and Cassius meekly accepts his decision to leave Cicero out of the conspiracy. He is more doubtful when Brutus—still idealistic—declares that Antony shall not be killed with Caesar, but he again allows himself to be overruled. The striking clock brings to an end the serious business of the meeting and, after a joke at the expense of Caesar, the conspirators leave Brutus to his thoughts.

Portia makes us remember the mental anguish that Brutus has endured. She is a character with whom we can sympathize, in her loving care for her husband, and whom we are intended to admire for her fortitude in bearing the wound in her thigh. Because of our feelings for Portia, we are sympathetic to the man she loves. There is no need, however, for the audience to hear what Brutus tells Portia about the conspiracy, so Shakespeare is able to show us a further example of the high regard in which the Romans hold Brutus—a 'Brave son, deriv'd from honourable loins'.

Scene 2   Like Casca, Calpurnia is distressed by the unnatural events of the night, and she has also had a frightening dream, which Caesar narrates to Decius Brutus. But Decius is determined to get Caesar to the Capitol, and his interpretation of the dream is flattering. Tempted with the thought of a crown, and also afraid of being laughed at, Caesar has made up his mind to go out when the conspirators come to escort him.

Scene 3   Another warning has been prepared for Caesar. Artemidorus reads his letter aloud, so that we shall know what is in the paper that Caesar refuses to read.

Scene 4   Portia is anxious. Brutus has told her of the conspiracy, and she knows the danger that her husband is in. The tension grows.

ACT 3

Scene 1   Caesar, accompanied by the conspirators (like armed guards to see that he does not escape from them), approaches the Capitol. He rejects the petition from Artemidorus, and goes towards the Senate House, where the senators are waiting for him. Brutus and Cassius stay at the back of the procession. There is a moment of panic for Cassius, but Brutus calms him down; and now everything goes according to plan. At the very moment when Caesar is speaking of his own constancy (which reflects the order and constancy in the universe), chaos breaks loose. Caesar is killed; the conspirators (whom we now see as anarchists) proclaim the death of tyranny; 'Men, wives and children stare, cry out and run | As it were doomsday'. Calpurnia's dream comes true when the conspirators, at Brutus's command, bathe their hands in Caesar's blood, congratulating themselves on having performed a deed which will be recorded in history.

Into this hysterical scene comes Antony's servant, calming the riot situation with his master's careful words, before Antony enters. At the beginning of this scene, Trebonius drew Antony aside, so that he did not go to the Capitol with Caesar; after the murder we hear that he has 'Fled to his house amaz'd'. Now he is very controlled. His speech to the conspirators sounds submissive, as though he were anxious to please them; but we ought not to ignore a possible irony in his address to them as 'gentlemen', nor a disgust in his reference to their 'purpled hands [that] do reek and smoke'. He is also perhaps ironic in describing them as 'The choice and master spirits of this age'—although we may not notice this until we read the play a second time, and know Antony's real feelings, which have not yet been made clear.

Antony shakes the hands of the murderers, taking note of their names; we remember that Brutus also shook the hands of the conspirators who came to his house, signifying his allegiance with them. Antony knows that he must be creating a bad impression that he is 'Either a coward or a flatterer'; but we must not be deceived by appearances. Brutus and Cassius contrast in their reception of Antony. Brutus welcomes him, sure that he will be a friend when he hears their explanations. Cassius, however, is still suspicious; he suggests a bribe, but he advises Brutus not to let Antony make the funeral oration. Once more, Brutus overrules Cassius.

Left alone on the stage, Antony shows that he is a loyal friend to Caesar—and a dangerous enemy to the conspirators. He prophesies the disasters that will follow Caesar's murder, and he has no sooner spoken than the first signs of impending war are apparent in the news that Octavius is coming to Rome. The movement of the play suddenly changes direction. Until now, everything has been aimed at the murder of Caesar; from this point, the aim is to secure revenge.

'Lend me your hand.' Antony asks the servant to help him carry Caesar's body off the stage. There were no curtains in the Elizabethan theatre, and competent dramatists ensured that after a murderous episode there were enough living characters on stage to remove the dead ones. Shakespeare was more than merely competent. Necessity demanded the introduction of another living character after Antony's prophetic speech, but Shakespeare makes a virtue out of necessity by having that character announce the coming of Octavius, so that the second movement of the play starts as soon as the first movement is completed.

Scene 2   The scene that follows invites us to make a contrast between two kinds of oratory, considered in terms of their effects on the citizens who hear the speeches. Brutus speaks in prose, trying to present a reasoned argument to justify the murder. The citizens are fairly satisfied with this, but it is ironic that they now wish to elevate Brutus into Caesar's place: they have not appreciated the principle behind Brutus's act. Antony's speech is in verse; there is no attempt to produce logical argument, for the oration—with its repetitions, rhetorical questions, ironies, and open display of emotion—is aimed at the hearts, and not the heads of the people. We see the citizens in the process of changing their minds every time that Antony makes a well-calculated pause in his speech. Antony takes care with his references to the conspirators: his first allusion to them as 'honourable men' seems quite straightforward, but with each repetition the phrase gathers irony. It is a citizen, not Antony himself, who finally gives words to Antony's meaning: 'They were traitors. Honourable men!' Antony cannot be faulted for his understanding of the psychology of crowds, and he easily achieves his desired end.

Scene 3 The black comedy of this scene serves to lighten the tension that built up during and after Antony's oration. At the same time, the scene shows how the movement to avenge Caesar's murder is gathering force; in Act 4 it has erupted into civil war.

ACT 4

Scene 1 Passion has now given place to cold calculation as the members of the new triumvirate decide that in the coming 'purge' neither brother nor nephew shall be spared. Antony's dismissal of Lepidus—'a slight unmeritable man'—casts a suspicion of trouble to come; but Shakespeare is content to let the matter rest here.

Scene 2 More immediately serious is the lack of harmony between Brutus and Cassius, which must be kept secret from their armies.

Scene 3 Once again Brutus shows his idealism, which is outraged by Cassius's conduct. But Brutus has another cause for grief—his wife is dead.

Two passages in this scene duplicate the information about Portia's death. Shakespeare probably wrote first the version given in lines 181–95, and then—perhaps thinking that he had made Brutus too much a Stoic—added the lines that now appear as 147–57; and forgot to cross out the first draft. The play was not printed until 1623, and the printer would not tamper with an author's manuscript, even though the author was dead. So both versions were printed.

A decision has to be made by the conspirators whether to march to Philippi and encounter the Roman army there; or whether to remain in their present position. Cassius gives good reasons for staying where they are, but once more Brutus overrules him. This will prove fatal—as we are assured by the appearance of Caesar's ghost, with its ominous promise to Brutus: 'thou shalt see me at Philippi'.

ACT 5

In the scenes that follow, the absence of fixed scenery becomes a positive advantage, as the action moves from one camp to the other, located generally on the battlefield at Philippi. With our modern sound-effects, the noise of soldiers marching and fighting, coming nearer and moving further away, would make a good background for the speeches.

Scene 1

The armies of Brutus and Cassius have advanced towards Philippi, and Octavius's surprise confirms our suspicion that Brutus made the wrong decision. The verbal clash between Antony and Octavius, on one side, and Brutus and Cassius on the other, is in part a substitute for the physical combat impossible on stage. Antony and Octavius are victorious here—just as they will be in the real fighting.

Alone with Messala, Cassius loses the confidence with which he had answered Antony. Cassius has little hope left, and his parting with Brutus is very moving. It seems that Shakespeare is now working to increase our sympathies for the former conspirators.

Scene 2
Scene 3

Now the fight has begun, and we hear from Brutus that things are going well with his soldiers. Cassius's army, however, has been overthrown, and a mistaken report of Brutus's situation causes him to despair. Defeated, he commits suicide. Titinius, finding the body, laments briefly; then kills himself, following Cassius's example in performing 'a Roman's part'. When Brutus comes upon the scene, he underlines the growing sense that Cassius was, after all, an honourable man and a true Roman: 'It is impossible that ever Rome | Should breed thy fellow'.

Scene 4

More skirmishes follow, and all the characters involved in them seem to be demonstrating their nobility: Young Cato dies bravely; Lucilius pretends to be Brutus in order to deceive the enemy soldiers; Antony is generous in his rescue and treatment of Lucilius.

Scene 5   But Brutus, in another part of the battlefield, recognizes that he is defeated. The friends that have gathered round him grieve, more for his sake than for their own; and Brutus rejoices in their loyalty when he finds that none of them will agree to his request and kill him. When at last he runs upon his sword, there is relief in his voice: 'Caesar, now be still, I I kill'd not thee with half so good a will'.

The conflict within Brutus—between love for Caesar and love for Rome—is at an end. His epitaph is spoken by Mark Antony, in terms that make us wonder whether Brutus, said to have been 'the noblest Roman of them all', was perhaps the true hero of Shakespeare's play, *Julius Caesar*.

Brutus—'the noblest Roman of them all'?

The superlative praise of Antony's description of Brutus has a powerful effect on our minds, especially since it comes so close to the climax of the action, and only a few lines from the end of the play. We are left to wonder whether Brutus is, in fact, the hero of *Julius Caesar*—or whether Antony's obituary notice is speaking the whole truth.

Shakespeare takes the character of Brutus, with very little alteration, from *The Lives of the Greeks and Romans*, where Plutarch described him as

> a marvellous lowly and gentle person, noble minded, and would never be in any rage, nor carried away with pleasure and covetousness; but had ever an upright mind with him, and would never yield to any wrong or injustice.

In the play we begin to form a good opinion of Brutus from what the other characters say of him. Cassius is the first to speak his praises, but he assures Brutus (and us) that 'many of the best respect in Rome' (1, 2, 59) similarly esteem him. A glowing tribute to Brutus is expressed by Casca:

> O, he sits high in all the people's hearts,
> And that which would appear offence in us
> His countenance, like richest alchemy,
> Will change to virtue and to worthiness.   (1, 3, 157–60)

From his mocking account of the ceremony with the crown (1, 2, 220ff.) we have seen that Casca is not a man who is easily impressed; consequently we value his praise more highly.

When we see Brutus himself on the stage, we are conscious most of all of the mental anguish that he is suffering, torn between personal love for Caesar and patriotic love for Rome. He does not wish to worry Cassius, but prefers, as he says, to 'turn the trouble of my countenance | Merely upon myself' (1, 2, 38–9). It is very much in his favour that Brutus is not immediately won by the persuasions of Cassius but, having listened to the arguments, asks for time to consider them (1, 2, 165–70). His soliloquy in *Act 2, Scene 1* confirms our opinion of his sense of responsibility, and our sympathies are moved when he tells us that since Cassius first spoke to him (which was four weeks earlier) he has not slept. Portia's account of his distressed behaviour also makes us feel sympathetic towards her husband, whilst Brutus's tenderness for his wife (and for the page, Lucius) is an attractive quality that we did not expect to find in a man with so much on his mind.

We have no doubts about Caesar's love for Brutus, although there is little time in the play for this to be demonstrated. It is enough that we hear the famous cry '*Et tu, Brute*' when Caesar discovers that his friend is one of the conspirators (3, 1, 77). Plutarch told how Caesar gave up the fight for his life when he recognized Brutus:

> Men report also that Caesar did still defend himself against the rest, running every way with his body. But when he saw Brutus with his sword drawn in his hand, then he pulled his gown over his head and made no more resistance.

We understand exactly what feelings were involved when Antony explains to the crowd:

> Brutus, as you know, was Caesar's angel.
> Judge, O you gods, how dearly Caesar lov'd him!
> This was the most unkindest cut of all.
> For when the noble Caesar saw him stab,
> Ingratitude, more strong than traitors' arms,
> Quite vanquish'd him. Then burst his mighty heart
>
> (3, 2, 179–84)

Brutus is always conscious of Caesar's love, and of the ingratitude with which he has repaid it. When he has been defeated, and runs on his sword to avoid being captured, he seems to welcome his death, almost as though it were a punishment for his offence in killing Caesar: 'Caesar now be still | I kill'd not thee with half so good a will' (5, 5, 50–1). Yet the needs of Rome, as Brutus understands them, are more important than the demands of friendship, and in his speech to the Roman people Brutus offers justification for his act: 'not that I loved Caesar less, but that I loved Rome more' (3, 2, 21–2).

Brutus is an idealist. He is descended from patriots, and he is often reminded of the Lucius Junius Brutus who drove Tarquin from Rome and helped to found the first republic. Brutus's motives for joining the conspiracy are wholly pure, and he intends to maintain this purity in everything: to swear an oath of allegiance between the conspirators would, he feels, 'stain | The even virtue of our enterprise' (2, 1, 132–3), casting a shadow of doubt both on the cause and on the men. He will not agree that Antony should be killed along with Caesar, because this would turn what he sees as ritual sacrifice into bloody butchery. Cassius argues against Brutus here, and also when Antony asks permission to address the citizens at Caesar's funeral. On both occasions Brutus's idealism is strong, and Cassius is overruled; events prove Cassius to have been right both times.

The contrast between the idealist, Brutus, and the realist, Cassius, is never more clearly shown than in their quarrel about money. The practical Cassius recognizes that, in time of war, 'it is not meet | That every nice offence should bear his comment' (4, 3, 7–8). Brutus, in a passion of honour, refuses to raise money by ignoble means, and says he would 'rather coin my heart | And drop my blood for drachmaes' (4, 3, 72–3). We cannot help feeling that this sentiment is very fine—but not much use for paying soldiers' wages.

The trouble with idealism is that it can so easily blind those who possess it—and Brutus is blinded. The conspiracy *might* have succeeded if Antony, as well as Caesar, had died on the ides of March. All *might* still have been well for the murderers if Antony had not been permitted to stir the citizens to mutiny with his funeral oration. And there might even have been some little chance of victory if Brutus had not insisted on marching to Philippi. But the biggest mistake that Brutus makes is his initial decision, arrived at with such difficulty, that Caesar has to die.

Brutus is wrong. It is easy to be influenced by a character so sympathetically drawn as Brutus undoubtedly is, and to accept that character's estimation of his own deeds. But when we read, very carefully, the soliloquy in the garden, it becomes plain that Brutus is deceiving himself. He confesses that he has 'no personal cause' to fear Caesar and, furthermore, that he has never known 'when his affections sway'd | More than his reason' (2, 1, 11, 20–1). Unable to fault Caesar from Caesar's own conduct, Brutus resorts to a generalization, a 'common proof' (2, 1, 21), which says that ambitious men, at the height of their power, scorn those beneath them. With no more justification than this, Brutus argues that Caesar is a potential tyrant and therefore must be killed. He himself admits that his argument is unacceptable— 'Will bear no colour for the thing he is'; and he attempts to rephrase it ('Fashion it thus') in a more convincing manner (2, 1, 29–30). He convinces himself—and patriotism does the rest.

It is patriotism, very largely, that leads Brutus into the trap laid for him by Cassius. Caesar shows shrewd judgement when he recognizes Cassius as one of those men who are 'never at heart's ease | Whiles they behold a greater than themselves' (1, 2, 208–9). Brutus is too innocent to see the danger that Caesar sees in Cassius, but Cassius himself admits it to the audience when he gloats over his success in manipulating the 'honourable mettle' of Brutus so that it is perverted from its true nature—'wrought | From that it is dispos'd' (1, 2, 307–8).

The tragedy of Brutus lies here—not that he attempted to free the republic of Rome from a tyrannous dictator and was killed in the action; but that, *with the best of motives,* he was responsible for the murder of

> the noblest man
> That ever lived in the tide of times.   (3, 1, 256–7)

Shakespeare's Verse

Easily the best way to understand and appreciate Shakespeare's verse is to read it aloud—and don't worry if you don't understand everything! Try not to be captivated by the dominant rhythm, but decide which are the most important words in each line and use the regular metre to drive them forward to the listeners. Shakespeare's plays are mainly written in 'blank verse', the form preferred by most dramatists in the sixteenth and early seventeenth centuries. It is a very flexible medium, which is capable—like the human speaking voice—of a wide range of tones. Basically the lines, which are unrhymed, are ten syllables long. The syllables have alternating stresses, just like normal English speech; and they divide into five 'feet'. The technical name for this is 'iambic pentameter'.

> **Murellus**
> You blócks, you stónes, you wórse than sénseless thíngs!
> O yoú hard heárts, you crúel mén of Róme,
> Knew yoú not Pómpey? Mány a tíme and óft
> Have yoú climb'd úp to wálls and báttleménts,
> To tówers and wíndows, yéa, to chímney-tóps,
> Your ínfants ín your árms, and thére have sát
> The lívelong dáy, with pátient éxpectátion,
> To seé great Pómpey páss the stréets of Róme.
> And whén you sáw his chário bút appeár
> Have yóu not máde an únivérsal shoút,
> That Tíber trémbled únderneáth her bánks
> To heár the réplicátion óf your soúnds
> Made ín her cóncave shóres?   *1, 1, 37–49*

In this quotation, the lines are regular in length and normal in iambic stress pattern. Two syllables have to be elided in 'Many a', and 'towers' must seem to be one syllable—but these are usual enough in spoken English. Sometimes Shakespeare deviates from the norm that he has set, writing lines that are longer or shorter than ten syllables, and varying the stress patterns for unusual emphasis. Here, for example, Murellus does not complete the pentameter in line 49; the character makes a dramatic pause so that his words can sink in to the hearers' consciousness.

The verse line sometimes contains the grammatical unit of meaning—'To see great Pompey pass the streets of Rome'—thus allowing for a pause at the end of the line, before a new idea is started; at other times, the sense runs on from one line to the next—'have sat The livelong day'. This makes for the natural fluidity of speech, avoiding monotony but still maintaining the iambic rhythm.

Source, Date, and Text

Shakespeare's main source for *Julius Caesar* was Plutarch's *Parallel Lives of the Greeks and Romans*; this was written in Greek in the first century AD, translated into French (by Jacques Amyot) in 1559, and from French into English (by Sir Thomas North) in 1575. North's translation gave Shakespeare the characters and plot outlines for four of his plays— *Julius Caesar, Antony and Cleopatra, Coriolanus*, and *Timon of Athens*— and Shakespeare so respected North's vigorous colloquial prose that he often retained its phraseology and idioms, making only slight adjustments for the purpose of rhythm and emphasis (see 'Shakespeare's Plutarch', p.106).

The play was probably written around 1599, and a Swiss visitor to England records a performance that he saw on 21 September 1599 'in the house with the thatched roof'—Shakespeare's Globe Theatre. It was not published until 1623, when it was printed in the First Folio collection of Shakespeare's *Works*.

The present edition uses the text established by Marvin Spevack for the New Cambridge Shakespeare (1998).

People in the Play

Julius Caesar

Octavius Caesar
Mark Antony   *triumvirs after the death of* Julius Caesar
Aemilius Lepidus

Cicero
Publius   *senators*
Popillius Lena

Marcus Brutus
Cassius
Casca
Trebonius
Ligarius   *conspirators against* Julius Caesar
Decius Brutus
Metellus Cimber
Cinna

Flavius
Murellus   *tribunes*

Artemidorus   *a schoolmaster*
Cinna   *a poet*

Lucilius
Titinius
Messala   *friends of* Brutus *and of* Cassius
Young Cato
Volumnius

Varrus
Clitus
Claudio
Strato
Lucius   *servants or officers attending* Brutus
Dardanius
Flavius
Labeo

Pindarus   *servant to* Cassius

Calpurnia   Caesar's *wife*

Portia   Brutus's *wife*

A Soothsayer
Another Poet
Senators, Citizens, Attendants, Soldiers

'*Enter* Caesar . . . *for the course*', (1, 2, Os.d.). Robert Stephens as Caesar, Royal Shakespeare Company, 1991.

ACT 1

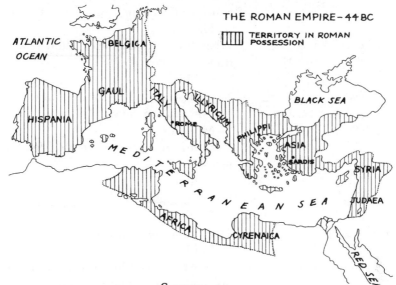

THE ROMAN EMPIRE – 44 BC

|||| TERRITORY IN ROMAN POSSESSION

ATLANTIC OCEAN
BELGICA
GAUL
HISPANIA
ITALY
ILLYRICUM
ROME
PHILIPPI
BLACK SEA
ASIA
SARDIS
SYRIA
JUDAEA
MEDITERRANEAN SEA
AFRICA
CYRENAICA
RED SEA

Act 1 Scene 1

The tribunes are angry because some tradesmen are taking a holiday to celebrate Julius Caesar's triumphant entry into Rome.

0s.d. *over the stage*: This direction indicates that the actors should walk from one side of the stage to the other.

1–5 *Hence . . . thou*: The verse immediately identifies the social class of the tribunes.

3 *mechanical*: manual labourers.

4–5 *the sign . . . profession*: the tools of your trade.

5 *thou*: This is the 'familiar' form of the pronoun, used (instead of 'you') to address inferiors, children, and intimates.

7 *rule*: ruler.

10 *in respect of*: in comparison with.

11 *cobbler*: shoe-repairer, clumsy workman.

SCENE 1

Rome: a street. Enter Flavius, Murellus, *and certain* Commoners *over the stage*

Flavius
Hence! Home, you idle creatures, get you home!
Is this a holiday? What, know you not,
Being mechanical, you ought not walk
Upon a labouring day without the sign
5 Of your profession? Speak, what trade art thou?
Carpenter
Why, sir, a carpenter.
Murellus
Where is thy leather apron and thy rule?
What dost thou with thy best apparel on?
You, sir, what trade are you?
Cobbler
10 Truly, sir, in respect of a fine workman, I am but, as you would say, a cobbler.
Murellus
But what trade art thou? Answer me directly.

13 *use*: practise.

14 *soles*: The Cobbler makes the common pun with 'souls'.

15 *naughty*: good-for-nothing, worthless; the word had a stronger meaning than in modern usage.

17–18 *you be out*: you are out of temper; your shoes are worn out.

18 *mend*: both 'patch your shoes' and 'improve your character'.

23 *awl*: a small pointed tool for piercing holes; an obvious pun with 'all' develops into sexual innuendo with the reference (line 24) to 'women's matters'.
meddle: interfere.

25 *withal*: nevertheless.

26 *recover*: repair—with a pun on 're-cover'.

26–7 *As . . . leather*: The expression was proverbial.

26 *proper*: fine.

27 *neat's leather*: cowhide, shoe leather.

33 *triumph*: triumphal procession bringing captives and spoils of battle into the city; Caesar is apparently returning from the battle of Munda (see 'About the Play', p.v).

35 *tributaries*: captured enemies, paying tribute-money.

36 *grace . . . bonds*: honour by appearing bound as captives.

37 *senseless things*: objects incapable of feeling or perception.

39 *Pompey*: Pompey had been allied with Caesar and Crassus in the first triumvirate (see 'About the Play', p.v).

41–2 *climbed . . . tops*: Shakespeare seems to be describing an Elizabethan scene.

Cobbler
A trade, sir, that I hope I may use with a safe conscience, which is indeed, sir, a mender of bad soles.
Flavius
15 What trade, thou knave? Thou naughty knave, what trade?
Cobbler
Nay, I beseech you, sir, be not out with me; yet if you be out, sir, I can mend you.
Murellus
What mean'st thou by that? Mend me, thou saucy
20 fellow?
Cobbler
Why, sir, cobble you.
Flavius
Thou art a cobbler, art thou?
Cobbler
Truly, sir, all that I live by is with the awl. I meddle with no tradesman's matters, nor women's matters; but
25 withal I am indeed, sir, a surgeon to old shoes: when they are in great danger I recover them. As proper men as ever trod upon neat's leather have gone upon my handiwork.
Flavius
But wherefore art not in thy shop today?
30 Why dost thou lead these men about the streets?
Cobbler
Truly, sir, to wear out their shoes, to get myself into more work. But indeed, sir, we make holiday to see Caesar and to rejoice in his triumph.
Murellus
Wherefore rejoice? What conquest brings he home?
35 What tributaries follow him to Rome
To grace in captive bonds his chariot wheels?
You blocks, you stones, you worse than senseless things!
O you hard hearts, you cruel men of Rome,
Knew you not Pompey? Many a time and oft
40 Have you climb'd up to walls and battlements,
To towers and windows, yea, to chimney tops,
Your infants in your arms, and there have sat

43 *the . . . day*: throughout the whole day.

45 *And when . . . appear*: as soon as you caught sight of his chariot.

46 *made an universal shout*: all shouted at once.

48 *replication*: re-echoing.

49 *concave shores*: overhanging river banks.

51 *cull*: pick, choose.

53 *Pompey's blood*: Pompey's two sons were defeated by Caesar at the battle of Munda.

56 *intermit*: delay.

57 *needs must light*: must inevitably fall.

58 *for this fault*: to atone for this offence.

59 *sort*: class, rank.

61 *channel*: river-bed.

61–2 *the lowest . . . all*: the lowest water-level floods up to the highest bank.

63 *their basest metal*: the cheap metal (i.e. lead) that they are made of; their most contemptible spirits. The pun with 'metal' is continued with 'guilt'/'gilt' in the next line.
mov'd: affected; caused to remove; melted.

65 *Capitol*: The temple of Jupiter on the Capitoline Hill.

The livelong day, with patient expectation,
To see great Pompey pass the streets of Rome.

45 And when you saw his chariot but appear
Have you not made an universal shout,
That Tiber trembled underneath her banks
To hear the replication of your sounds
Made in her concave shores?

50 And do you now put on your best attire?
And do you now cull out a holiday?
And do you now strew flowers in his way,
That comes in triumph over Pompey's blood?
Be gone!

55 Run to your houses, fall upon your knees,
Pray to the gods to intermit the plague
That needs must light on this ingratitude.

Flavius
Go, go, good countrymen, and for this fault *Blood in*
Assemble all the poor men of your sort, *Calpurnia's*
dream
60 Draw them to Tiber banks, and weep your tears
Into the channel till the lowest stream
Do kiss the most exalted shores of all.

[*Exeunt all the* Commoners

See where their basest metal be not mov'd:
They vanish tongue-tied in their guiltiness.

65 Go you down that way towards the Capitol,

66–7 *Disrobe . . . ceremonies*: It would
  be sacrilege to desecrate the statues
  in this way.
67 *ceremonies*: ceremonial vestments.
69 *feast of Lupercal*: A feast day in
  honour of the fertility god Lupercus
  was held on 15 February. Shakespeare
  has accelerated the action of the play
  by merging the triumphant return from
  Munda (October 45 BC) into the
  events of spring 42 BC.
71 *trophies*: arms, spoils taken from
  captured enemies.
  I'll about: I will walk about.
72 *the vulgar*: the common people.
74–5 *These . . . pitch*: restraining these
  early enthusiasms will make him less
  of a highflier; the image is of plucking
  feathers from a young falcon's wing.
75 *pitch*: height (of a falcon's flight).

Act 1 Scene 2
Caesar's procession crosses the stage on
the way to the ceremonial games. Brutus
and Cassius linger behind, and Cassius
hints of future danger. The procession
returns, and Casca describes Caesar's
refusal of the crown. Brutus arranges to
meet Cassius again, and Cassius explains
his tactics to the audience.

Os.d. *for the course*: prepared for the
  race. On the feast of Lupercal
  (see *1*, 1, 69), young men ran naked
  through the city, touching spectators
  with leather thongs; see
  'Shakespeare's Plutarch', p.106.

3 *Antonio*: Shakespeare's actors were
  probably more familiar with this
  Italian form of the name than with the
  Latin *Antonius*.

7 *elders*: wise men.
8 *touched*: touchèd.
9 *sterile curse*: curse of sterility.

This way will I. Disrobe the images
If you do find them deck'd with ceremonies.
    Murellus
May we do so?
You know it is the feast of Lupercal.
    Flavius
70 It is no matter; let no images
Be hung with Caesar's trophies. I'll about
And drive away the vulgar from the streets;
So do you too, where you perceive them thick.
These growing feathers pluck'd from Caesar's wing
75 Will make him fly an ordinary pitch,
Who else would soar above the view of men
And keep us all in servile fearfulness.   *[Exeunt*

SCENE 2

Rome: a public place. Enter Caesar, Antony *for the
course,* Calpurnia, Portia, Decius, Cicero, Brutus,
Cassius, Casca, *a* Soothsayer, *a great crowd
following; after them* Murellus *and* Flavius

    Caesar
Calpurnia.
    Casca
              Peace ho, Caesar speaks.
    Caesar
                             Calpurnia.
    Calpurnia
Here, my lord.
    Caesar
Stand you directly in Antonio's way
When he doth run his course. Antonio.
    Antony
5 Caesar, my lord.
    Caesar
Forget not in your speed, Antonio,
To touch Calpurnia, for our elders say
The barren, touched in this holy chase,
Shake off their sterile curse.

Antony
I shall remember:
10 When Caesar says, 'Do this', it is perform'd.
Caesar

Set on, and leave no ceremony out.
Soothsayer
Caesar!
Caesar
Ha? Who calls?
Casca
Bid every noise be still—peace yet again!
Caesar
15 Who is it in the press that calls on me?
I hear a tongue shriller than all the music
Cry 'Caesar!' Speak, Caesar is turn'd to hear.
Soothsayer
Beware the Ides of March.
Caesar
What man is that?
Brutus
A soothsayer bids you beware the Ides of March.
Caesar
20 Set him before me, let me see his face.
Cassius
Fellow, come from the throng, look upon Caesar.
Caesar
What say'st thou to me now? Speak once again.
Soothsayer
Beware the Ides of March.
Caesar
He is a dreamer, let us leave him. Pass.

Sennet

Exeunt all but Brutus *and* Cassius

Cassius
25 Will you go see the order of the course?
Brutus
Not I.
Cassius
I pray you, do.

11 *Set on*: proceed.

15 *press*: crowd.

18 *Ides of March*: 15 March.

24 *Sennet*: trumpet fanfare signalling the departure of the procession.

25 *order*: ritualistic proceeding.

28 *gamesome*: inclined to make merry.
29 *quick*: lively, frivolous.

32 *of late*: recently.

34 *wont*: accustomed.
35 *You . . . hand*: you are too assertive in this unfriendly ('strange') manner.

37 *I . . . look*: I haven't shown my feelings.

39 *Merely*: entirely.
   Vexed: vexèd.
40 *passions . . . difference*: greatly conflicting emotions.
41 *Conceptions . . . myself*: ideas concerning nobody but myself.
42 *give . . . behaviours*: have an adverse effect on my conduct.
43 *griev'd*: worried.

48 *passion*: feelings.
49–50 *By means . . . cogitations*: because of this I have kept to myself some serious thoughts, ideas worth thinking about.

53 *But by . . . things*: except when it is reflected in something else.

54 *just*: exact.

56 *turn*: reflect.

58 *shadow*: reflection.
59 *best respect*: highest importance.
60 *immortal*: Cassius speaks ironically.

Brutus
I am not gamesome: I do lack some part
Of that quick spirit that is in Antony.
30 Let me not hinder, Cassius, your desires;
I'll leave you.
   Cassius
Brutus, I do observe you now of late:
I have not from your eyes that gentleness
And show of love as I was wont to have.
35 You bear too stubborn and too strange a hand
Over your friend that loves you.
   Brutus
                                           Cassius,
Be not deceiv'd. If I have veil'd my look
I turn the trouble of my countenance
Merely upon myself. Vexed I am
40 Of late with passions of some difference,
Conceptions only proper to myself,
Which give some soil, perhaps, to my behaviours.
But let not therefore my good friends be griev'd
(Among which number, Cassius, be you one)
45 Nor construe any further my neglect
Than that poor Brutus, with himself at war,
Forgets the shows of love to other men.
   Cassius
Then, Brutus, I have much mistook your passion,
By means whereof this breast of mine hath buried
50 Thoughts of great value, worthy cogitations.
Tell me, good Brutus, can you see your face?
   Brutus
No, Cassius, for the eye sees not itself
But by reflection, by some other things.
   Cassius
'Tis just,
55 And it is very much lamented, Brutus,
That you have no such mirrors as will turn
Your hidden worthiness into your eye
That you might see your shadow. I have heard
Where many of the best respect in Rome
60 (Except immortal Caesar), speaking of Brutus

61 *this age's yoke*: the oppression of these times.

62 *had his eyes*: had the speaker's eyes (to see himself as others see him); would use his eyes (to see things as the speaker does).

66 *Therefore*: for that reason.

69 *modestly*: without exaggeration. *discover*: reveal.

71 *jealous on*: suspicious of. *gentle*: noble.

72 *laughter*: subject of jest, laughing-stock.

72–4 *did use . . . protester*: were in the habit of cheapening my friendship by promising it to every new acquaintance who says he wants to be friends with me.

75 *fawn on*: make myself agreeable to.

76 *scandal*: slander.

77–8 *That . . . rout*: that when I've had a few drinks I declare myself pals with the whole crowd.

78 *hold*: consider.

78s.d. *Flourish*: trumpet fanfare.

85 *toward*: concerning. *general*: public.

87 *indifferently*: unconcernedly.

88 *speed*: prosper.

91 *favour*: appearance.

And groaning underneath this age's yoke,
Have wish'd that noble Brutus had his eyes.
    Brutus
Into what dangers would you lead me, Cassius,
That you would have me seek into myself
65 For that which is not in me?
    Cassius
Therefore, good Brutus, be prepar'd to hear.
And since you know you cannot see yourself
So well as by reflection, I, your glass,
Will modestly discover to yourself
70 That of yourself which you yet know not of.
And be not jealous on me, gentle Brutus,
Were I a common laughter, or did use
To stale with ordinary oaths my love
To every new protester. If you know
75 That I do fawn on men and hug them hard
And after scandal them, or if you know
That I profess myself in banqueting
To all the rout, then hold me dangerous.

    Flourish and shout

    Brutus
What means this shouting? I do fear the people
80 Choose Caesar for their king.
    Cassius
                                Ay, do you fear it?
Then must I think you would not have it so.
    Brutus
I would not, Cassius, yet I love him well.
But wherefore do you hold me here so long?
What is it that you would impart to me?
85 If it be aught toward the general good,
Set honour in one eye and death i'th'other
And I will look on both indifferently.
For let the gods so speed me as I love
The name of honour more than I fear death.
    Cassius
90 I know that virtue to be in you, Brutus,
As well as I do know your outward favour.

Well, honour is the subject of my story:
I cannot tell what you and other men
Think of this life, but for my single self
95 I had as lief not be as live to be
In awe of such a thing as I myself.
I was born free as Caesar, so were you;
We both have fed as well, and we can both
Endure the winter's cold as well as he.
100 For once, upon a raw and gusty day,
The troubled Tiber chafing with her shores,
Caesar said to me, 'Dar'st thou, Cassius, now
Leap in with me into this angry flood
And swim to yonder point?' Upon the word,
105 Accoutred as I was, I plunged in
And bade him follow; so indeed he did.
The torrent roar'd, and we did buffet it
With lusty sinews, throwing it aside
And stemming it with hearts of controversy.
110 But ere we could arrive the point propos'd,
Caesar cried, 'Help me, Cassius, or I sink!'
Ay, as Aeneas, our great ancestor,
Did from the flames of Troy upon his shoulder
The old Anchises bear, so from the waves of Tiber
115 Did I the tired Caesar. And this man
Is now become a god, and Cassius is
A wretched creature and must bend his body
If Caesar carelessly but nod on him.
He had a fever when he was in Spain,
120 And when the fit was on him I did mark
How he did shake. 'Tis true, this god did shake,
His coward lips did from their colour fly,
And that same eye whose bend doth awe the world
Did lose his lustre. I did hear him groan,
125 Ay, and that tongue of his that bade the Romans
Mark him and write his speeches in their books,
'Alas', it cried, 'give me some drink, Titinius',
As a sick girl. Ye gods, it doth amaze me
A man of such a feeble temper should
130 So get the start of the majestic world
And bear the palm alone.

Shout. Flourish

---

95 *had as lief*: would rather.
96 *such . . . myself*: someone who is just a man like myself.

101 *chafing . . . shores*: raging against the restraint of the shores.

105 *Accoutred*: fully dressed.
plunged: plungèd.
107 *buffet*: contend with.
108–9 *throwing . . . controversy*: thrusting it aside and rising above it with competitive spirits (competing against the tide, and against each other).
112–14 *Aeneas . . . bear*: Aeneas, the legendary founder of Rome, escaped from the ruined city of Troy, carrying his father on his back; the story is told in Virgil's *Aeneid*.
117 *bend his body*: bow.
118 *carelessly*: casually.
119–21 *He had . . . shake*: Julius Caesar in fact suffered from epilepsy, and Plutarch describes how this 'took him the first time . . . in Corduba, a city of Spain'—but Plutarch is insistent that Caesar 'yielded not to the sickness of his body, to make it a cloak to cherish him withal, but, contrarily, took the pains of war as a medicine to cure his sick body, fighting always with his disease'.
122 *His . . . fly*: i.e. he went white; Cassius implies that cowardice, not sickness, caused Caesar's pallor.
123 *bend*: glance.
124 *his*: its.
125–6 *that tongue . . . books*: 'Caesar had an excellent natural gift to speak well before the people' (Plutarch).
127 *Titinius*: Cassius refers to Titinius as 'my best friend' (5, 3, 35).
129 *temper*: constitution.
130 *get . . . world*: get ahead of the world in the race for power (majesty).
131 *bear . . . palm*: carry off the victor's crown of palm leaves.

Brutus
Another general shout!
I do believe that these applauses are
For some new honours that are heap'd on Caesar.
Cassius
135 Why, man, he doth bestride the narrow world
Like a Colossus, and we petty men
Walk under his huge legs and peep about
To find ourselves dishonourable graves.
Men at some time are masters of their fates:
140 The fault, dear Brutus, is not in our stars
But in ourselves, that we are underlings.
Brutus and Caesar: what should be in that 'Caesar'?
Why should that name be sounded more than yours?
Write them together, yours is as fair a name;
145 Sound them, it doth become the mouth as well;
Weigh them, it is as heavy; conjure with 'em,
'Brutus' will start a spirit as soon as 'Caesar'.
Now in the names of all the gods at once,
Upon what meat doth this our Caesar feed
150 That he is grown so great? Age, thou art sham'd!
Rome, thou hast lost the breed of noble bloods!
When went there by an age since the great flood
But it was fam'd with more than with one man?
When could they say, till now, that talk'd of Rome,
155 That her wide walks encompass'd but one man?

132 *general*: from all the people.

136 *Colossus*: i.e. the statue of Apollo which was traditionally said to span the entrance to the harbour at Rhodes.

140 *our stars*: our horoscopes, the positions of the stars when we were born.
141 *underlings*: inferior servants.

145 *Sound*: utter.
146 *conjure with 'em*: use them to invoke spirits.
147 *start*: raise up.
150 *Age*: Cassius addresses the present time.
151 *noble bloods*: valiant and honourable men.
152 *the great flood*: According to classical mythology, this was sent by Zeus as punishment for the sins of humankind; only one man and his wife were saved from destruction.
153 *fam'd with*: famous for.
155 *wide walks*: spacious territories.
encompass'd: held.

159 *There . . . once*: The present Brutus
claims to be descended from Lucius
Junius Brutus, the traditional founder
of the Roman Republic in the sixth
century BC; see *2, 1, 53–4*note.
brook'd: tolerated.
160 *eternal*: eternally damned.
keep his state: maintain his kingdom.
161 *easily*: readily.
162 *am nothing jealous*: do not doubt in
the least.
163 *work*: persuade.
have some aim: can make a guess.
165–7 *For this . . . us*: for the
moment—if I can ask you as a
friend—I would rather not be urged
any further.
170 *meet*: suitable.
high: important.
171 *chew upon*: think about.
172–5 *Brutus . . . us*: Brutus would rather
be a peasant than call himself a
Roman citizen under the oppression
that's likely to arise in these days.
177 *have . . . fire*: have struck just this
little appearance of enthusiasm;
Cassius compares his words to steel
striking upon flint.

178 *train*: band of followers.
180 *after . . . fashion*: in his cynical
manner.
181 *worthy note*: worth taking note of.
184 *chidden*: scolded.
185 *Cicero*: A great Roman orator and
statesman.
186 *ferret . . . eyes*: blazingly angry eyes
(like those of a ferret hunting rats).
188 *cross'd in conference*: opposed in
discussion, countered in argument.

Now is it Rome indeed and room enough
When there is in it but one only man.
O, you and I have heard our fathers say
There was a Brutus once that would have brook'd
160 Th'eternal devil to keep his state in Rome
As easily as a king.

Brutus
That you do love me, I am nothing jealous;
What you would work me to, I have some aim.
How I have thought of this, and of these times,
165 I shall recount hereafter. For this present,
I would not (so with love I might entreat you)
Be any further mov'd. What you have said
I will consider; what you have to say
I will with patience hear and find a time
170 Both meet to hear and answer such high things.
Till then, my noble friend, chew upon this:
Brutus had rather be a villager
Than to repute himself a son of Rome
Under these hard conditions as this time
175 Is like to lay upon us.

Cassius
I am glad that my weak words
Have struck but thus much show of fire from Brutus.

Enter Caesar *and his train*

Brutus
The games are done and Caesar is returning.

Cassius
As they pass by, pluck Casca by the sleeve
180 And he will (after his sour fashion) tell you
What hath proceeded worthy note today.

Brutus
I will do so. But look you, Cassius,
The angry spot doth glow on Caesar's brow
And all the rest look like a chidden train:
185 Calpurnia's cheek is pale, and Cicero
Looks with such ferret and such fiery eyes
As we have seen him in the Capitol,
Being cross'd in conference by some senators.

Cassius

Casca will tell us what the matter is.

Caesar

190 Antonio.

Antony

Caesar.

Caesar

Let me have men about me that are fat,

Sleek-headed men and such as sleep a-nights.

Yond Cassius has a lean and hungry look,

195 He thinks too much: such men are dangerous.

Antony

Fear him not, Caesar, he's not dangerous,

He is a noble Roman and well given.

Caesar

Would he were fatter! But I fear him not.

Yet if my name were liable to fear

200 I do not know the man I should avoid

So soon as that spare Cassius. He reads much,

He is a great observer, and he looks

Quite through the deeds of men. He loves no plays,

As thou dost, Antony, he hears no music;

205 Seldom he smiles, and smiles in such a sort

As if he mock'd himself and scorn'd his spirit

That could be mov'd to smile at any thing.

Such men as he be never at heart's ease

Whiles they behold a greater than themselves,

210 And therefore are they very dangerous.

I rather tell thee what is to be fear'd

Than what I fear: for always I am Caesar.

Come on my right hand, for this ear is deaf,

And tell me truly what thou think'st of him.

Sennet

Exeunt Caesar *and his train*

Casca

215 You pull'd me by the cloak, would you speak with me?

Brutus

Ay, Casca, tell us what hath chanc'd today

That Caesar looks so sad.

---

193 *Sleek-headed*: agreeable, well-disposed; see 'Shakespeare's Plutarch', p.105.

194 *Yond Cassius*: that man Cassius over there.

197 *well given*: with a good reputation.

199 *if . . . fear*: if I had any tendency to be afraid.

201 *spare*: skinny.

202–3 *he looks . . . men*: he can see right through the things that men do (and understand their motives).

205 *sort*: way.

206–7 *scorn'd . . . thing*: despised any man who could be persuaded to smile for any reason.

208 *at heart's ease*: fully contented.

213 *this . . . deaf*: This detail is Shakespeare's own invention.

215 *would you*: do you want to.

216 *chanc'd*: happened.

217 *sad*: serious.

Casca

Why, you were with him, were you not?

Brutus

I should not then ask, Casca, what had chanc'd.

Casca

220 Why, there was a crown offered him, and being offered him he put it by with the back of his hand thus, and then the people fell a-shouting.

Brutus

What was the second noise for?

Casca

Why, for that too.

Cassius

225 They shouted thrice; what was the last cry for?

Casca

Why, for that too.

Brutus

Was the crown offered him thrice?

Casca

Ay, marry, was't, and he put it by thrice, every time gentler than other; and at every putting-by mine honest
230 neighbours shouted.

Cassius

Who offered him the crown?

Casca

Why, Antony.

Brutus

Tell us the manner of it, gentle Casca.

Casca

I can as well be hanged as tell the manner of it. It was
235 mere foolery, I did not mark it. I saw Mark Antony offer him a crown—yet 'twas not a crown neither, 'twas one of these coronets—and, as I told you, he put it by once; but for all that, to my thinking he would fain have had it. Then he offered it to him again; then he put it by
240 again; but to my thinking he was very loath to lay his fingers off it. And then he offered it the third time; he put it the third time by, and still as he refused it, the rabblement hooted, and clapped their chopped hands, and threw up their sweaty nightcaps, and uttered such a
245 deal of stinking breath because Caesar refused the

221 *put it by*: pushed it away.

228 *Ay . . . was't*: yes indeed it was; 'marry' (= by the Virgin Mary) is a very mild oath.
229–30 *mine honest neighbours*: the simple-minded creatures around me.

235 *did not mark it*: took no notice of it.

238 *would fain have*: would like to have.

242 *still*: always.
243 *rabblement*: mob.
hooted: shouted.
chopped: chapped.
244 *nightcaps*: soft caps (worn by day and night).

247 *swounded*: fainted.

250 *soft*: wait a minute.

253 *like*: likely.
falling sickness: epilepsy; see
119–21 note.

257 *the tag-rag people*: the rabble
(dressed in 'tags and rags').

259 *use*: are accustomed.
264 *plucked me ope*: went and tore open;
'me' is used here for greater
emphasis.
doublet: close-fitting tunic worn by
Elizabethan gentlemen; contemporary
performances of Shakespeare's plays
were always in such 'modern' dress.

265 *And*: if.
man of any occupation: craftsman,
tradesman; soldier.
266 *at a word*: at his word (and done what
he told me to do).
269 *amiss*: wrong.
272 *there's . . . them*: you can't take any
notice of them.

crown that it had, almost, choked Caesar, for he
swounded and fell down at it. And for mine own part I
durst not laugh for fear of opening my lips and
receiving the bad air.
    Cassius
250 But soft, I pray you; what, did Caesar swound?
    Casca
He fell down in the market-place, and foamed at
mouth, and was speechless.
    Brutus
'Tis very like, he hath the falling sickness.
    Cassius
No, Caesar hath it not, but you, and I,
255 And honest Casca, we have the falling sickness.
    Casca
I know not what you mean by that, but I am sure Caesar
fell down. If the tag-rag people did not clap him and
hiss him according as he pleased and displeased them,
as they use to do the players in the theatre, I am no true
260 man.
    Brutus
What said he when he came unto himself?
    Casca
Marry, before he fell down, when he perceived the
common herd was glad he refused the crown, he
plucked me ope his doublet and offered them his throat
265 to cut. And I had been a man of any occupation, if I
would not have taken him at a word I would I might go
to hell among the rogues. And so he fell. When he came
to himself again, he said if he had done or said anything
amiss, he desired their worships to think it was his
270 infirmity. Three or four wenches where I stood cried,
'Alas, good soul', and forgave him with all their hearts.
But there's no heed to be taken of them: if Caesar had
stabbed their mothers they would have done no less.
    Brutus
And after that he came thus sad away?
    Casca
275 Ay.
    Cassius
Did Cicero say anything?

277 *he spoke Greek*: Plutarch said that Cicero was always cautious in speech—and that he had a habit of expressing witticisms in Greek.
278 *effect*: purpose.

279 *and*: if.

282 *Greek to me*: Casca uses a catchphrase meaning 'I could make no sense of it'.
284 *put to silence*: This may be a cynical euphemism for 'executed'; Plutarch says they were 'deprived . . . of their tribuneships'.

287 *am promised forth*: have promised to eat out (away from home).

288 *dine*: have dinner (the main meal, eaten at midday by Romans and by Elizabethans).
289 *your mind hold*: you have not changed your mind.

294 *quick mettle*: lively, energetic.

295 *execution*: performance.

297 *However . . . form*: despite this languid appearance he assumes.
298 *rudeness*: roughness.
wit: intelligence.
299–300 *gives . . . appetite*: makes men more inclined to think about what he is saying (just as a sauce brings out the flavour of the meat).

Casca
Ay, he spoke Greek.
Cassius
To what effect?
Casca
Nay, and I tell you that, I'll ne'er look you i'th'face again.
280 But those that understood him smiled at one another
and shook their heads; but for mine own part it was
Greek to me. I could tell you more news too. Murellus
and Flavius, for pulling scarves off Caesar's images, are
put to silence. Fare you well. There was more foolery
285 yet, if I could remember it.
Cassius
Will you sup with me tonight, Casca?
Casca
No, I am promised forth.
Cassius
Will you dine with me tomorrow?
Casca
Ay, if I be alive, and your mind hold, and your dinner
290 worth the eating.
Cassius
Good, I will expect you.
Casca
Do so. Farewell both.   [*Exit*
Brutus
What a blunt fellow is this grown to be!
He was quick mettle when he went to school.
Cassius
295 So is he now in execution
Of any bold or noble enterprise,
However he puts on this tardy form.
This rudeness is a sauce to his good wit,
Which gives men stomach to digest his words
300 With better appetite.
Brutus
And so it is. For this time I will leave you.
Tomorrow if you please to speak with me,
I will come home to you; or if you will,
Come home to me and I will wait for you.

Soliloquy

Cassius

305 I will do so. Till then, think of the world.   [*Exit* Brutus

Well, Brutus, thou art noble; yet I see

Thy honourable metal may be wrought

From that it is dispos'd. Therefore it is meet

That noble minds keep ever with their likes;

310 For who so firm that cannot be seduc'd?

Caesar doth bear me hard, but he loves Brutus.

If I were Brutus now and he were Cassius,

He should not humour me. I will this night,

In several hands, in at his windows throw,

315 As if they came from several citizens,

Writings, all tending to the great opinion

That Rome holds of his name, wherein obscurely

Caesar's ambition shall be glanced at.

And after this let Caesar seat him sure,

320 For we will shake him, or worse days endure.   [*Exit*

Act 1 Scene 3

A terrible storm is raging; Casca describes some unnatural happenings, but Cicero is unimpressed. Cassius, rejoicing in the weather and the omens, tells Casca that he hopes Brutus will join the rebels.

SCENE 3

Rome: a street. Thunder and lightning. Enter from opposite sides Casca *and* Cicero

Cicero

Good even, Casca, brought you Caesar home?

Why are you breathless, and why stare you so?

Casca

Are not you mov'd when all the sway of earth

Shakes like a thing unfirm? O Cicero,

5 I have seen tempests when the scolding winds

Have riv'd the knotty oaks, and I have seen

Th'ambitious ocean swell, and rage, and foam,

To be exalted with the threatening clouds;

But never till tonight, never till now,

10 Did I go through a tempest dropping fire.

Either there is a civil strife in heaven,

Or else the world, too saucy with the gods,

Incenses them to send destruction.

---

305 *the world*: the state of affairs.

307 *metal*: Cassius makes the usual pun with 'mettle'.
wrought: twisted.

308 *From . . . dispos'd*: out of its natural shape.

308–9 *it is meet . . . likes*: it's important that men of integrity should always keep together.

310 *firm*: resolute, strong-minded.

311 *bear me hard*: has difficulty in putting up with me.

313 *should . . . me*: would not be able to influence me (i.e. as Cassius is going to work on Brutus).

313–16 *I will . . . Writings*: tonight I will throw through Brutus's windows some letters, written in different ('several') handwritings, as though they came from different people.

316 *tending*: alluding.

317 *obscurely*: indirectly.

318 *glanced*: glancèd; hinted.

319 *seat him sure*: be certain of his position.

1 *even*: evening.
brought . . . home: did you escort Caesar to his house.

3 *sway*: realm.

4 *unfirm*: unsteady.

6 *riv'd*: torn.
knotty: knotted.

7 *ambitious*: i.e. the ocean seemed to want to overreach its bounds.

8 *exalted with*: raised up to.

10 *dropping fire*: raining down lightning and thunderbolts.

11 *civil strife in heaven*: civil war between the gods.

12 *saucy*: insolent.

13 *Incenses*: angers (literally, 'fires').

Cicero

Why, saw you anything more wonderful?

Casca

15   A common slave—you know him well by sight—
Held up his left hand, which did flame and burn
Like twenty torches join'd, and yet his hand,
Not sensible of fire, remain'd unscorch'd.
Besides—I ha' not since put up my sword—
20   Against the Capitol I met a lion
Who glaz'd upon me and went surly by
Without annoying me. And there were drawn
Upon a heap a hundred ghastly women,
Transformed with their fear, who swore they saw
25   Men, all in fire, walk up and down the streets.
And yesterday the bird of night did sit
Even at noon-day upon the market-place,
Hooting and shrieking. When these prodigies
Do so conjointly meet let not men say,
30   'These are their reasons, they are natural',
For I believe they are portentous things
Unto the climate that they point upon.

Cicero

Indeed, it is a strange-disposed time.
But men may construe things after their fashion
35   Clean from the purpose of the things themselves.
Comes Caesar to the Capitol tomorrow?

Casca

He doth, for he did bid Antonio
Send word to you he would be there tomorrow.

Cicero

Good night then, Casca. This disturbed sky
40   Is not to walk in.

Casca

Farewell, Cicero.   [*Exit* Cicero

---

18 *Not sensible of*: not feeling.

20 *Against*: in front of.
21 *glaz'd*: glared.
22 *annoying*: injuring.
22–3 *drawn Upon a heap*: huddled into a group.
23 *ghastly*: looking like ghosts.
24 *Transformed*: transformèd.

26 *the bird of night*: the owl.

28 *prodigies*: extraordinary events.
29 *conjointly*: all together.
30 *reasons*: causes.
31 *portentous*: ominous.
32 *climate*: region.
    that . . . upon: at which they are directed.
33 *a strange-disposed time*: disposèd; a time in which strange things are happening.
34 *construe*: interpret.
35 *Clean from*: quite contrary to.

39 *disturbed*: disturbèd.

Enter Cassius

Cassius
Who's there?
Casca
                    A Roman.
Cassius
                                        Casca, by your voice.
Casca
Your ear is good. Cassius, what night is this!
Cassius
A very pleasing night to honest men.
Casca
Who ever knew the heavens menace so?
Cassius
45 Those that have known the earth so full of faults.
    For my part I have walk'd about the streets,
    Submitting me unto the perilous night,
    And, thus unbraced, Casca, as you see,
    Have bar'd my bosom to the thunderstone;
50 And when the cross blue lightning seem'd to open
    The breast of heaven, I did present myself
    Even in the aim and very flash of it.
        Casca
    But wherefore did you so much tempt the heavens?
    It is the part of men to fear and tremble
55 When the most mighty gods by tokens send
    Such dreadful heralds to astonish us.
        Cassius
    You are dull, Casca, and those sparks of life
    That should be in a Roman you do want,
    Or else you use not. You look pale, and gaze,
60 And put on fear, and cast yourself in wonder
    To see the strange impatience of the heavens.
    But if you would consider the true cause
    Why all these fires, why all these gliding ghosts,
    Why birds and beasts from quality and kind,
65 Why old men, fools, and children calculate,
    Why all these things change from their ordinance,
    Their natures, and preformed faculties,
    To monstrous quality—why, you shall find

42 *what night*: what a night.

47 *Submitting me*: exposing myself.
48 *unbraced*: unbracèd; with clothing
    loosened or unfastened.
49 *thunderstone*: thunderbolt.
50 *cross*: zigzag.

52 *Even in the aim*: just where it was
    directed.
53 *tempt*: test.
54 *part*: duty.

55 *tokens*: signs.

56 *heralds*: omens, foretelling disaster.
    astonish: dismay.

57 *dull*: stupid.
58 *want*: lack.
59 *use not*: do not make use of them.

61 *impatience*: restlessness.

64 *from . . . kind*: depart from their usual
    natures.
65 *calculate*: reckon things up.
66 *ordinance*: ordained behaviour.
67 *preformed faculties*: preformèd;
    qualities with which they were born.
68 *monstrous quality*: unnatural
    behaviour.

69 *infus'd . . . spirits*: poured these
powers into them.

71 *Unto . . . state*: about some unnatural
state of affairs.

That heaven hath infus'd them with these spirits
70 To make them instruments of fear, and warning
Unto some monstrous state.
Now could I, Casca, name to thee a man
Most like this dreadful night,
That thunders, lightens, opens graves, and roars
75 As doth the lion in the Capitol—
A man no mightier than thyself, or me,
In personal action, yet prodigious grown
And fearful, as these strange eruptions are.

77 *In personal action*: in what he can do
himself.
prodigious: monstrous, ominous.
78 *fearful*: frightening.
eruptions: outbreaks.

    Casca
'Tis Caesar that you mean, is it not, Cassius?
    Cassius
80 Let it be who it is, for Romans now
Have thews and limbs like to their ancestors'.
But, woe the while, our fathers' minds are dead
And we are govern'd with our mothers' spirits;
Our yoke and sufferance show us womanish.
    Casca
85 Indeed, they say the senators tomorrow
Mean to establish Caesar as a king,
And he shall wear his crown by sea and land,
In every place save here in Italy.

81 *thews*: sinews.
like to: similar to.
82 *woe the while*: alas for these times.

84 *Our . . . sufferance*: our patient
endurance of this oppression.

85–8 *the senators . . . Italy*: Their past
history had taught Romans to fear
dictators, and although they would
allow Caesar to rule the Empire, they
refused to give him absolute power in
Italy.

Cassius

I know where I will wear this dagger then:
90 Cassius from bondage will deliver Cassius.
Therein, ye gods, you make the weak most strong;
Therein, ye gods, you tyrants do defeat.
Nor stony tower, nor walls of beaten brass,
Nor airless dungeon, nor strong links of iron,
95 Can be retentive to the strength of spirit;
But life, being weary of these worldly bars,
Never lacks power to dismiss itself.
If I know this, know all the world besides,
That part of tyranny that I do bear
100 I can shake off at pleasure.

Thunder still

Casca
                                    So can I,
So every bondman in his own hand bears
The power to cancel his captivity.
Cassius
And why should Caesar be a tyrant then?
Poor man, I know he would not be a wolf
105 But that he sees the Romans are but sheep;
He were no lion, were not Romans hinds.
Those that with haste will make a mighty fire
Begin it with weak straws. What trash is Rome,
What rubbish and what offal, when it serves
110 For the base matter to illuminate
So vile a thing as Caesar? But, O grief,
Where hast thou led me? I perhaps speak this
Before a willing bondman, then I know
My answer must be made. But I am arm'd,
115 And dangers are to me indifferent.
Casca
You speak to Casca, and to such a man
That is no fleering tell-tale. Hold, my hand.
Be factious for redress of all these griefs,
And I will set this foot of mine as far
120 As who goes farthest.

95 *Can . . . spirit*: can confine the resolution of the spirit.
96 *worldly bars*: restrictions of this world.
97 *dismiss*: free.

99 *That . . . bear*: the tyranny as it affects me.

101 *bondman*: slave, prisoner.
102 *cancel*: destroy the bond (a legal term).

106 *were no lion*: would not be a lion.
  hinds: deer; peasants.
108 *trash*: brushwood, twigs.
109 *offal*: fallen chips of wood.
110 *base matter*: material from which the fire is started.
  illuminate: light up, set fire to.

115 *indifferent*: unimportant.

117 *fleering*: scornful.
  Hold, my hand: here, let's shake hands (as a token of unity).
118 *Be . . . griefs*: form a party (faction) to get these grievances put right.
119–20 *I will . . . farthest*: I will go with you as far as anyone can.

Cassius

There's a bargain made.
Now know you, Casca, I have mov'd already
Some certain of the noblest-minded Romans
To undergo with me an enterprise
Of honourable dangerous consequence.
125 And I do know by this they stay for me
In Pompey's Porch. For now, this fearful night,
There is no stir or walking in the streets,
And the complexion of the element
In favour's like the work we have in hand,
130 Most bloody, fiery, and most terrible.

Enter Cinna

Casca
Stand close a while, for here comes one in haste.
Cassius   *walk*
'Tis Cinna, I do know him by his gait.
He is a friend. Cinna, where haste you so?
Cinna
To find you out. Who's that? Metellus Cimber?
Cassius
135 No, it is Casca, one incorporate
To our attempts. Am I not stay'd for, Cinna?
Cinna
I am glad on't. What a fearful night is this!
There's two or three of us have seen strange sights.
Cassius
Am I not stay'd for? Tell me.
Cinna

Yes, you are.
140 O Cassius, if you could
But win the noble Brutus to our party—
Cassius
Be you content. Good Cinna, take this paper
And look you lay it in the *Judge* praetor's chair,
Where Brutus may but find it; and throw this
145 In at his window; set this up with wax
Upon old Brutus' statue. All this done,
Repair to Pompey's Porch, where you shall find us.

121 *know you*: let me tell you.
  mov'd: persuaded.
122 *Some certain*: certain individuals.

124 *Of . . . consequence*: which will be dangerous, but whose outcome will be honourable.
125 *by this*: by this time.
  stay: are waiting.
126 *Pompey's Porch*: The Porch was adjacent to Pompey's Theatre (the first permanent theatre built—55 BC—in Rome) and was intended as a shelter for spectators.

128 *complexion of the element*: condition of the sky.
129 *In favour's*: in appearance is.
131 *Stand close*: keep hidden.
132 *gait*: walk.
134 *find . . . out*: look for.
135–6 *incorporate . . . attempts*: united with us in our undertaking.
136 *stay'd for*: waited for.
137 *on't*: of it.

143 *praetor*: magistrate; Brutus was appointed to this high position by Caesar in 44 BC.
144 *Where . . . it*: where only Brutus can find it; where Brutus cannot but find it.
145 *set . . . wax*: fasten it with wax.
146 *old Brutus*: Junius Brutus (see note to 1, 2, 159).
  all this done: when all this has been done.
147 *Repair*: make your way.

Is Decius Brutus and Trebonius there?
   Cinna
All but Metellus Cimber, and he's gone
150 To seek you at your house. Well, I will hie,
And so bestow these papers as you bade me.
   Cassius
That done, repair to Pompey's Theatre.   [*Exit* Cinna
Come, Casca, you and I will yet, ere day,
See Brutus at his house. Three parts of him
155 Is ours already, and the man entire
Upon the next encounter yields him ours.
   Casca
O, he sits high in all the people's hearts,
And that which would appear offence in us
His countenance, like richest alchemy,
160 Will change to virtue and to worthiness.
   Cassius
Him and his worth and our great need of him
You have right well conceited. Let us go,
For it is after midnight, and ere day
We will awake him and be sure of him.   [*Exeunt*

150 *hie*: hurry.
151 *bestow*: distribute.

155–6 *the man . . . ours*: next time we meet him, we'll get him entirely over to our side.

157 *sits high*: is highly esteemed.
158 *offence*: criminal.
159 *countenance*: approval.
alchemy: the 'science' that tried to change base metals (such as lead and tin) into gold.

162 *conceited*: understood and expressed.
163 *ere*: before.

ACT 2

Act 2 Scene 1
Brutus finds a letter urging him to action,
and Cassius introduces other conspirators.
Portia tries to restrain her husband, but
Ligarius gives fresh encouragement.

2 *by . . . stars*: from the positions of the
stars (the sky is still clouded from the
storm).
4 *I would . . . soundly*: I wish I could be
blamed for sleeping so soundly.

7 *taper*: candle.

10 *It . . . death*: he will have to be killed;
Brutus speaks from a train of thought
started before the opening of this
scene, attempting to justify the
murder of Caesar.
11 *spurn at*: kick against.
13 *that*: i.e. being crowned king.
14–15 *It is . . . walking*: on a sunny day
the snake will come out—and you
must walk carefully.
15 *Crown him that*: crown him king.
16 *I grant*: I agree (with Cassius).
put . . . him: give him power to do
injury.
18–19 *Th'abuse . . . power*: when
greatness is misused it separates
mercy from power.
20 *affections*: emotions.
sway'd: ruled.
21 *a common proof*: a well-known fact.
22 *lowliness . . . ladder*: when a man's
ambition starts to climb, the ones
below him become his ladder.
24 *upmost round*: top rung (of the
ladder).

SCENE 1

Rome: Brutus's garden. Enter Brutus *in his orchard.*

Brutus
What, Lucius, ho!
I cannot by the progress of the stars
Give guess how near to day. Lucius, I say!
I would it were my fault to sleep so soundly.
5 When, Lucius, when? Awake, I say! What, Lucius!

Enter Lucius

Lucius
Call'd you, my lord?
   Brutus
Get me a taper in my study, Lucius.
When it is lighted, come and call me here.
   Lucius
I will, my lord.   [*Exit*
   Brutus
10 It must be by his death. And for my part
I know no personal cause to spurn at him
But for the general. He would be crown'd:
How that might change his nature, there's the question.
It is the bright day that brings forth the adder
15 And that craves wary walking. Crown him that,
And then I grant we put a sting in him
That at his will he may do danger with.
Th'abuse of greatness is when it disjoins
Remorse from power. And to speak truth of Caesar,
20 I have not known when his affections sway'd
More than his reason. But 'tis a common proof
That lowliness is young ambition's ladder,
Whereto the climber-upward turns his face;
But when he once attains the upmost round

26 *degrees*: rungs, steps.

28–9 *the quarrel . . . he is*: I can't offer any bogus grounds for complaint ('colour') in what he is now.
30 *Fashion it thus*: look at it this way.
30–1 *that . . . extremities*: that his present nature, given increased power, would lead him into such and such excesses (of tyranny).
33 *as his kind*: according to his nature.
mischievous: harmful.

35 *closet*: study.
36 *window*: windowsill.
flint: i.e. to strike a light with.

40 *Is . . . Ides of March*: Shakespeare wants his audience to be aware of the passage of time.

44 *exhalations*: meteors (the unnatural storm is still raging).

49 *instigations*: calls to action.
50 *took*: picked.

25 He then unto the ladder turns his back,
Looks in the clouds, scorning the base degrees
By which he did ascend. So Caesar may.
Then lest he may, prevent. And since the quarrel
Will bear no colour for the thing he is,
30 Fashion it thus: that what he is, augmented,
Would run to these and these extremities.
And therefore think him as a serpent's egg
(Which, hatch'd, would as his kind grow mischievous)
And kill him in the shell.

Enter Lucius

Lucius
35 The taper burneth in your closet, sir.
Searching the window for a flint, I found
This paper, thus seal'd up, and I am sure
It did not lie there when I went to bed.

Gives him the letter

Brutus
Get you to bed again, it is not day.
40 Is not tomorrow, boy, the Ides of March?
Lucius
I know not, sir.
Brutus
Look in the calendar and bring me word.
Lucius
I will, sir.   [*Exit*
Brutus
The exhalations whizzing in the air
45 Give so much light that I may read by them.

Opens the letter and reads

'Brutus, thou sleep'st. Awake, and see thyself!
Shall Rome, etc. Speak, strike, redress!'
'Brutus, thou sleep'st. Awake!'
Such instigations have been often dropp'd
50 Where I have took them up.

51 *piece it out*: fill the gaps.

52 *under . . . awe*: in fear of one man.

53–4 *My ancestors . . . king*: Brutus claimed descent from Lucius Junius Brutus, who overthrew Tarquinius Superbus (534–510 BC), the last king of Rome; see *1, 2, 159*.

55 *redress*: reform, amend.

58 *Thy full petition*: everything you are asking for.

59 *fifteen*: Lucius includes the day that is just dawning in his reckoning of time that has passed ('is wasted').

59s.d *within*: offstage.

60 *'Tis good*: Perhaps Brutus is thanking his servant—or perhaps he is relieved that the Ides of March has come at last.

61 *whet*: sharpen (like a knife), incite.

63–5 *Between . . . dream*: The interval ('interim') between the first suggestion ('motion') and the performance ('acting') of a terrible deed is like a nightmare or a horrid dream.

66–9 *The genius . . . insurrection*: the spirit is then in conference with human faculties, and the man's whole being is disturbed—just as a kingdom is upset by civil war; Brutus uses a popular Elizabethan metaphor.

66 *genius*: The Romans believed that everybody had a tutelary god or guiding spirit.

70 *your brother*: Cassius was married to Brutus's sister.

72 *mo*: more.

'Shall Rome, etc.' Thus must I piece it out:
Shall Rome stand under one man's awe? What, Rome?
My ancestors did from the streets of Rome
The Tarquin drive when he was call'd a king.
55 'Speak, strike, redress!' Am I entreated
To speak and strike? O Rome, I make thee promise,
If the redress will follow, thou receivest
Thy full petition at the hand of Brutus.

Enter Lucius

Lucius
Sir, March is wasted fifteen days.

Knock within

Brutus
60 'Tis good. Go to the gate, somebody knocks.

[*Exit* Lucius

Since Cassius first did whet me against Caesar
I have not slept.
Between the acting of a dreadful thing
And the first motion, all the interim is
65 Like a phantasma or a hideous dream.
The genius and the mortal instruments
Are then in council, and the state of a man,
Like to a little kingdom, suffers then
The nature of an insurrection.

Enter Lucius

Lucius
70 Sir, 'tis your brother Cassius at the door,
Who doth desire to see you.
Brutus
                                            Is he alone?
Lucius
No, sir, there are mo with him.
Brutus
                                            Do you know them?

Lucius
No, sir, their hats are pluck'd about their ears
And half their faces buried in their cloaks,
75 That by no means I may discover them
By any mark of favour.

Brutus
Let 'em enter.   [*Exit* Lucius
They are the faction. O conspiracy,
Sham'st thou to show thy dang'rous brow by night,
When evils are most free? O then by day
80 Where wilt thou find a cavern dark enough
To mask thy monstrous visage? Seek none, conspiracy,
Hide it in smiles and affability,
For if thou path, thy native semblance on,
Not Erebus itself were dim enough
85 To hide thee from prevention.

Enter the conspirators, Cassius, Casca, Decius,
Cinna, Metellus, *and* Trebonius

Cassius
I think we are too bold upon your rest.
Good morrow, Brutus, do we trouble you?

Brutus
I have been up this hour, awake all night.
Know I these men that come along with you?

Cassius
90 Yes, every man of them; and no man here
But honours you, and every one doth wish
You had but that opinion of yourself
Which every noble Roman bears of you.
This is Trebonius.

Brutus
He is welcome hither.

Cassius
95 This, Decius Brutus.

Brutus
He is welcome too.

Cassius
This, Casca; this, Cinna; and this, Metellus Cimber.

74 *their . . . cloaks*: Shakespeare imagines his characters in Elizabethan costume.

75 *discover*: identify.
76 *favour*: appearance.
77 *faction*: party of conspirators.
79 *free*: common.
83 *path . . . on*: go on your way showing your real face.
84 *Erebus*: A name given to the classical underworld, hell.
85 *prevention*: being anticipated and frustrated.
86 *bold upon*: presumptuous in interrupting.
88 *this hour*: for an hour.

Brutus
They are all welcome.
What watchful cares do interpose themselves
Betwixt your eyes and night?
　　Cassius
100　Shall I entreat a word?

They whisper

Decius
Here lies the east, doth not the day break here?
　　Casca
No.
　　Cinna
O, pardon, sir, it doth, and yon grey lines
That fret the clouds are messengers of day.
　　Casca
105　You shall confess that you are both deceiv'd.
Here, as I point my sword, the sun arises,
Which is a great way growing on the south,
Weighing the youthful season of the year.
Some two months hence, up higher toward the north
110　He first presents his fire, and the high east
Stands, as the Capitol, directly here.
　　Brutus
[*Advancing with* Cassius] Give me your hands all over,
　　one by one.
　　Cassius
And let us swear our resolution.
　　Brutus
No, not an oath! If not the face of men,
115　The sufferance of our souls, the time's abuse—
If these be motives weak, break off betimes,
And every man hence to his idle bed;
So let high-sighted tyranny range on,
Till each man drop by lottery. But if these
120　(As I am sure they do) bear fire enough
To kindle cowards and to steel with valour
The melting spirits of women, then, countrymen,
What need we any spur but our own cause
To prick us to redress? What other bond

98–9 *What . . . night*: what problems are keeping you awake (forcing themselves between your eyes and sleep).

100 *entreat a word*: Cassius draws Brutus aside for some private conversation.

104 *fret*: streak.

106 *as*: according as.
107 *growing . . . south*: further south.
108 *Weighing*: considering.

110–11 *the high east . . . here*: due east is over here, where the Capitol stands.

112 *all over*: all included, every one of you.

114–16 *If . . . betimes*: if the sight of men's faces, our mental suffering, and the corruption of the age are not strong enough motives, we ought to give up at once ('betimes').
117 *idle bed*: bed of idleness.
118 *high-sighted tyranny*: tyranny that looks down from a great height.
range on: roam at large (like a beast in search of prey).
119 *lottery*: chance; it was the Roman practice, in a general mutiny, to punish certain soldiers, selected by lottery.
these: i.e. the conspirators.
120 *bear fire*: are spirited.
121 *kindle*: set aflame.
124 *prick*: urge.
redress: put things right.

125 *secret*: trustworthy.
    spoke the word: given our promise.
126 *palter*: cheat.
127 *honesty to honesty*: one honest man to another.
    engag'd: promised.
128 *this . . . it*: we will succeed or die.
129 *Swear priests*: let priests swear.
    men cautelous: men who are over-cautious.
130 *carrions*: men who have no more life in them than carcasses.
    suffering: patient, all-enduring.
131–2 *unto . . . doubt*: they are bad causes that are sworn to by untrustworthy men.
133 *even*: just, impartial.

138 *a several bastardy*: a separate act of baseness.

140 *that . . . him*: that he has given.

141 *sound him*: find out what he thinks.

142 *stand . . . us*: support us strongly.

144–6 *silver . . . deeds*: Metellus sees Cicero's age and experience in monetary terms.

148 *no whit*: not at all.

150 *break with*: confide in.

---

125 Than secret Romans that have spoke the word
And will not palter? And what other oath
Than honesty to honesty engag'd
That this shall be or we will fall for it?
Swear priests and cowards and men cautelous,
130 Old feeble carrions, and such suffering souls
That welcome wrongs: unto bad causes swear
Such creatures as men doubt. But do not stain
The even virtue of our enterprise
Nor th'insuppressive mettle of our spirits,
135 To think that or our cause or our performance
Did need an oath, when every drop of blood
That every Roman bears, and nobly bears,
Is guilty of a several bastardy
If he do break the smallest particle
140 Of any promise that hath pass'd from him.
    Cassius
But what of Cicero? Shall we sound him?
I think he will stand very strong with us.
    Casca
Let us not leave him out.
    Cinna
                        No, by no means.
    Metellus
O, let us have him, for his silver hairs
145 Will purchase us a good opinion
And buy men's voices to commend our deeds.
It shall be said his judgement rul'd our hands;
Our youths and wildness shall no whit appear,
But all be buried in his gravity.
    Brutus
150 O, name him not, let us not break with him,
For he will never follow anything
That other men begin.
    Cassius
                    Then leave him out.
    Casca
Indeed he is not fit.
    Decius
Shall no man else be touch'd but only Caesar?

155 *well urg'd*: a good idea.

157 *of him*: in him.
158 *shrewd*: keen.
    contriver: plotter.
    means: resources.
159 *improve*: make the most of.
160 *annoy*: injure.

162 *course*: course of action.

164 *envy*: malice.

167 *We . . . Caesar*: we oppose what
    Caesar represents (i.e. tyranny).

169 *come by*: take possession of.

175 *subtle*: crafty.
176 *Stir up*: incite.
177-8 *make . . . necessary*: make it seem
    that we did only what was necessary.
179 *Which . . . eyes*: when it looks like this
    to the common people.
180 *purgers*: surgeons (who treated
    patients by drawing off—purging—
    infected blood).

184 *ingrafted*: deeply rooted.

187 *to himself*: against himself.
    take thought: take it to heart.
188 *that . . . should*: that is too much to
    ask from him.

Cassius
155 Decius, well urg'd. I think it is not meet
Mark Antony, so well belov'd of Caesar,
Should outlive Caesar. We shall find of him
A shrewd contriver. And, you know, his means,
If he improve them, may well stretch so far
160 As to annoy us all, which to prevent,
Let Antony and Caesar fall together.
    Brutus
Our course will seem too bloody, Caius Cassius,
To cut the head off and then hack the limbs—
Like wrath in death and envy afterwards—
165 For Antony is but a limb of Caesar.
Let's be sacrificers, but not butchers, Caius.
We all stand up against the spirit of Caesar,
And in the spirit of men there is no blood.
O, that we then could come by Caesar's spirit
170 And not dismember Caesar! But, alas,
Caesar must bleed for it. And, gentle friends,
Let's kill him boldly, but not wrathfully;
Let's carve him as a dish fit for the gods,
Not hew him as a carcass fit for hounds.
175 And let our hearts, as subtle masters do,
Stir up their servants to an act of rage
And after seem to chide 'em. This shall make
Our purpose necessary, and not envious;
Which so appearing to the common eyes,
180 We shall be called purgers, not murderers.
And for Mark Antony, think not of him,
For he can do no more than Caesar's arm
When Caesar's head is off.
    Cassius
                    Yet I fear him,
For in the engrafted love he bears to Caesar—
    Brutus
185 Alas, good Cassius, do not think of him.
If he love Caesar, all that he can do
Is to himself—take thought and die for Caesar;
And that were much he should, for he is given
To sports, to wildness, and much company.

190 *no fear in*: nothing to fear from.

Trebonius
190 There is no fear in him, let him not die,
For he will live and laugh at this hereafter.

191s.d. *Clock strikes*: The striking clock is anachronistic—but important for building up the suspense of the scene.

Clock strikes

Brutus
Peace, count the clock.
    Cassius
                                The clock hath stricken three.
    Trebonius
'Tis time to part.
    Cassius
                    But it is doubtful yet
Whether Caesar will come forth today or no,

195 *he . . . late*: recently he has become superstitious.
196 *Quite*: very different.
    main: strong.
197 *ceremonies*: ritual prediction of the future.
198 *apparent prodigies*: wonders that have appeared.
200 *augurers*: soothsayers, priests who interpreted the omens.
201 *hold*: keep.

195 For he is superstitious grown of late,
Quite from the main opinion he held once
Of fantasy, of dreams, and ceremonies.
It may be these apparent prodigies,
The unaccustom'd terror of this night,
200 And the persuasion of his augurers
May hold him from the Capitol today.
    Decius
Never fear that. If he be so resolv'd

203 *o'ersway him*: make him change his mind.
204–6 *unicorns . . . toils*: Popular beliefs told of a unicorn that was caught when it drove its horn into a tree behind which the hunter was hiding, and of bears confused by their own reflections in looking-glasses; that elephants could be tempted into hidden pitfalls, and that lions might be trapped in nets ('toils').
208 *flattered*: flatterèd.
210 *I can . . . bent*: I know how to turn his mood the right way.

I can o'ersway him, for he loves to hear
That unicorns may be betray'd with trees,
205 And bears with glasses, elephants with holes,
Lions with toils, and men with flatterers.
But when I tell him he hates flatterers
He says he does, being then most flattered.
Let me work:
210 For I can give his humour the true bent,
And I will bring him to the Capitol.
        Cassius
Nay, we will all of us be there to fetch him.
        Brutus
By the eighth hour, is that the uttermost?
        Cinna

213 *uttermost*: very latest time.

Be that the uttermost, and fail not then.

Metellus

215 Caius Ligarius doth bear Caesar hard,
Who rated him for speaking well of Pompey.
I wonder none of you have thought of him.

Brutus

Now, good Metellus, go along by him.
He loves me well, and I have given him reasons.

220 Send him but hither and I'll fashion him.

Cassius

The morning comes upon's. We'll leave you, Brutus,
And, friends, disperse yourselves, but all remember
What you have said and show yourselves true Romans.

Brutus

Good gentlemen, look fresh and merrily:

225 Let not our looks put on our purposes,
But bear it as our Roman actors do,
With untir'd spirits and formal constancy.
And so good morrow to you every one.

[Exeunt all but Brutus

Boy! Lucius! Fast asleep? It is no matter,

230 Enjoy the honey-heavy dew of slumber.
Thou hast no figures nor no fantasies
Which busy care draws in the brains of men,
Therefore thou sleep'st so sound.

Enter Portia

Portia

Brutus, my lord.

Brutus

Portia! What mean you? Wherefore rise you now?

235 It is not for your health thus to commit
Your weak condition to the raw cold morning.

Portia

Nor for yours neither. Y'have ungently, Brutus,
Stole from my bed; and yesternight at supper
You suddenly arose and walk'd about,

240 Musing and sighing, with your arms across,
And when I ask'd you what the matter was,
You star'd upon me with ungentle looks.

215 *does . . . hard*: has a grudge against Caesar.
216 *rated*: reproved.

218 *by him*: by way of his house.
219 *reasons*: i.e. for mistrusting Caesar.
220 *fashion him*: persuade him to join us.

225 *put on*: take on the same appearance as.
226 *bear it*: carry it off.
227 *untir'd*: unflagging.
formal constancy: usual dignified behaviour.

230 *honey-heavy . . . slumber*: refreshing sweetness of deep sleep.
231 *figures*: problems.
fantasies: imaginings.
232 *busy*: restless.
draws: creates.

234 *what mean you*: what do you want.
235 *not for*: not good for.
commit: expose.
236 *weak condition*: delicate health.

237 *ungently*: unkindly.

240 *across*: folded.

245 *Yet*: still.
246 *wafture*: wave.

249 *enkindled*: provoked.
withal: also.
250 *an effect of humour*: caused by some passing mood.
251 *sometime . . . man*: affects everybody at some time.
his: its.
253–5 *could . . . you*: if it could alter your appearance as much as it has changed your disposition, I would not recognize you.
256 *your . . . grief*: the cause of your anxiety.

259 *embrace . . . it*: welcome some way to get better.

261 *physical*: good for your health.
262 *unbraced*: unbracèd; in loose clothing.
suck up: breathe in.
humours: vapours.
263 *dank*: cold and damp.
265 *dare . . . night*: risk catching some horrible infection carried on the night air.
266 *rheumy . . . air*: air which will give you catarrh because it has not yet been purified by the sun.
unpurged: unpurgèd.
268 *sick offence*: harmful disorder.
269 *place*: position (as your wife).
271 *charm*: entreat (in the name of some great power).
272 *that great vow*: i.e. the marriage vow.
273 *incorporate*: combine us into one body.
274 *unfold*: disclose.
275 *heavy*: solemn.
276 *had resort*: visited.

278 *Even from darkness*: although it was dark.

I urg'd you further, then you scratch'd your head
And too impatiently stamp'd with your foot.
245 Yet I insisted, yet you answer'd not,
But with an angry wafture of your hand
Gave sign for me to leave you. So I did,
Fearing to strengthen that impatience
Which seem'd too much enkindled, and withal
250 Hoping it was but an effect of humour
Which sometime hath his hour with every man.
It will not let you eat nor talk nor sleep;
And could it work so much upon your shape
As it hath much prevail'd on your condition,
255 I should not know you, Brutus. Dear my lord,
Make me acquainted with your cause of grief.
        Brutus
I am not well in health, and that is all.
        Portia
Brutus is wise, and were he not in health
He would embrace the means to come by it.
        Brutus
260 Why, so I do. Good Portia, go to bed.
        Portia
Is Brutus sick? And is it physical
To walk unbraced and suck up the humours
Of the dank morning? What, is Brutus sick?
And will he steal out of his wholesome bed
265 To dare the vile contagion of the night
And tempt the rheumy and unpurged air
To add unto his sickness? No, my Brutus,
You have some sick offence within your mind,
Which by the right and virtue of my place
270 I ought to know of. And upon my knees
I charm you, by my once commended beauty,
By all your vows of love, and that great vow
Which did incorporate and make us one,
That you unfold to me, your self, your half,
275 Why you are heavy and what men tonight
Have had resort to you, for here have been
Some six or seven who did hide their faces
Even from darkness.

Brutus

        Kneel not, gentle Portia.

    Portia

I should not need if you were gentle Brutus.

280 Within the bond of marriage, tell me, Brutus,

Is it excepted I should know no secrets

That appertain to you? Am I your self

But, as it were, in sort or limitation,

To keep with you at meals, comfort your bed,

285 And talk to you sometimes? Dwell I but in the suburbs

Of your good pleasure? If it be no more

Portia is Brutus' harlot, not his wife.

    Brutus

You are my true and honourable wife,

As dear to me as are the ruddy drops

290 That visit my sad heart.

    Portia

If this were true, then should I know this secret.

I grant I am a woman, but withal

A woman that Lord Brutus took to wife.

I grant I am a woman, but withal

295 A woman well reputed, Cato's daughter.

Think you I am no stronger than my sex,

Being so father'd and so husbanded?

Tell me your counsels, I will not disclose 'em.

I have made strong proof of my constancy,

300 Giving myself a voluntary wound

Here, in the thigh. Can I bear that with patience

And not my husband's secrets?

    Brutus

        O ye gods,

Render me worthy of this noble wife!

Knock

Hark, hark, one knocks. Portia, go in a while

305 And by and by thy bosom shall partake

The secrets of my heart.

All my engagements I will construe to thee,

All the charactery of my sad brows.

Leave me with haste.   [*Exit* Portia

Notes:

280–5 *Within . . . sometimes*: Portia playfully questions her legal status as Brutus's wife.
281 *Is it excepted*: is there some exception.
282 *appertain*: belong.
283 *in . . . limitation*: in some particular manner or limited period.
284 *keep with*: accompany.
285 *suburbs*: outskirts; in Elizabethan London the brothels were situated in the suburbs, and this leads to Portia's conclusion in line 287.
289 *drops*: i.e. of blood.
290 *visit*: The Elizabethans thought that blood was made in the liver, and flowed from there to the heart.
292 *grant*: admit. *withal*: in addition to that.
293 *took to wife*: married.
295 *well reputed*: with a good reputation. *Cato*: A Republican who fought for Pompey in the civil war and committed suicide to avoid being captured by Caesar.
296 *my sex*: other women.
298 *counsels*: private or secret purposes.
299 *constancy*: firmness, resolution.
305 *bosom*: heart. *partake*: share.
307 *engagements*: commitments. *construe*: explain.
308 *the . . . brows*: the reasons for my serious expression; 'Character' was the name coined in 1558 for a system of shorthand.

Lucius, who's that knocks?

Enter Lucius *and* Ligarius

Lucius
310 Here is a sick man that would speak with you.
　　Brutus
　　Caius Ligarius, that Metellus spake of.
　　Boy, stand aside.　　　　　　　　　　[*Exit* Lucius
　　　　　　　　　　Caius Ligarius, how?
　　Ligarius
　　Vouchsafe good morrow from a feeble tongue.
　　Brutus
　　O, what a time have you chose out, brave Caius,
315 To wear a kerchief! Would you were not sick!
　　Ligarius
　　I am not sick if Brutus have in hand
　　Any exploit worthy the name of honour.
　　Brutus
　　Such an exploit have I in hand, Ligarius,
　　Had you a healthful ear to hear of it.
　　Ligarius
320 By all the gods that Romans bow before,
　　I here discard my sickness! [*He pulls off his kerchief*]
　　　　Soul of Rome,
　　Brave son, deriv'd from honourable loins,
　　Thou, like an exorcist, hast conjur'd up
　　My mortified spirit. Now bid me run
325 And I will strive with things impossible,
　　Yea, get the better of them. What's to do?
　　Brutus
　　A piece of work that will make sick men whole.
　　Ligarius
　　But are not some whole that we must make sick?
　　Brutus
　　That must we also. What it is, my Caius,
330 I shall unfold to thee as we are going
　　To whom it must be done.

312 *how*: what does this mean.

313 *Vouchsafe*: graciously accept.

315 *kerchief*: scarf—i.e. to be ill.

319 *Had . . . it*: if you were well enough to hear it.

322 *deriv'd*: descended.
loins: ancestors.
323 *exorcist*: one who controls spirits by his magical commandments (conjuring).
324 *mortified*: mortifièd; dead.

327 *whole*: hale, healthy.

330 *unfold*: disclose.

331 *Set . . . foot*: get started.

332 *new fir'd*: with renewed energy.

333 *it sufficeth*: it is enough.

334s.d. *Thunder*: The sudden clap of thunder reminds the audience of the storm with which the scene started— and sounds an ominous warning for Caesar.

Act 2 Scene 2
Caesar's wife tries to dissuade him from going out when the omens are unfavourable, but Decius Brutus is scornful, and the conspirators escort Caesar to the Capitol.

0s.d. *nightgown*: dressing-gown.

3 *Who's within*: Caesar calls for a servant.

5 *present*: at once.

6 *success*: the result.

8 *What mean you*: what do you think you are doing.

10 *shall forth*: shall go out.

11 *Ne'er . . . back*: only ever saw my back.

12 *vanished*: vanishèd.

Ligarius
                             Set on your foot,
And with a heart new fir'd I follow you
To do I know not what; but it sufficeth
That Brutus leads me on.

Thunder

Brutus
                          Follow me then.   [*Exeunt*

SCENE 2

Rome: Caesar's house. Thunder and lightning. Enter Julius Caesar in his nightgown

Caesar
Nor heaven nor earth have been at peace tonight.
Thrice hath Calpurnia in her sleep cried out,
'Help ho, they murder Caesar!' Who's within?

Enter a Servant

Servant
My lord?
Caesar
5 Go bid the priests do present sacrifice
And bring me their opinions of success.
Servant
I will, my lord.   [*Exit*

Enter Calpurnia

Calpurnia
What mean you, Caesar, think you to walk forth?
You shall not stir out of your house today.
Caesar
10 Caesar shall forth. The things that threaten'd me
Ne'er look'd but on my back; when they shall see
The face of Caesar they are vanished.

13 *ceremonies*: outward forms.
14 *fright*: frighten.
  one within: someone in the house.

16 *watch*: night watchman (policeman).
17 *whelped*: whelpèd; given birth.
18 *yawn'd*: opened.

20 *squadrons*: soldiers arranged in square formations.
  right . . . war: correct battle order.
22 *hurtled*: clashed.

25 *beyond all use*: most unnatural.

27 *purpos'd*: ordained.

29 *Are . . . Caesar*: relate to the world in general as well as to Caesar.

31 *blaze forth*: flash out (in fiery meteors).

32–3 *Cowards . . . once*: Proverbial: 'A coward dies [in imagination] many deaths, a brave man but one'.

36 *necessary*: inevitable.
37 *augurers*: special priests who inspected the entrails of the sacrificial beast and interpreted the omens.

Calpurnia
Caesar, I never stood on ceremonies,
Yet now they fright me. There is one within,
15 Besides the things that we have heard and seen,
Recounts most horrid sights seen by the watch.
A lioness hath whelped in the streets,
And graves have yawn'd and yielded up their dead;
Fierce fiery warriors fight upon the clouds
20 In ranks and squadrons and right form of war,
Which drizzl'd blood upon the Capitol;
The noise of battle hurtled in the air,
Horses did neigh and dying men did groan,
And ghosts did shriek and squeal about the streets.
25 O Caesar, these things are beyond all use,
And I do fear them.
Caesar
                    What can be avoided
Whose end is purpos'd by the mighty gods?
Yet Caesar shall go forth, for these predictions
Are to the world in general as to Caesar.
Calpurnia
30 When beggars die there are no comets seen,
The heavens themselves blaze forth the death of princes.
Caesar
Cowards die many times before their deaths,
The valiant never taste of death but once.
Of all the wonders that I yet have heard
35 It seems to me most strange that men should fear,
Seeing that death, a necessary end,
Will come when it will come.

Enter a Servant

What say the augurers?

39 *offering*: animal sacrificed to the gods.

41 *in . . . cowardice*: to make cowards ashamed.

44 *Danger*: Caesar sees danger as a person.

46 *litter'd*: born.

49 *consum'd in*: eaten up by. *confidence*: over-confidence.

56 *for thy humour*: to satisfy your whim.

59 *fetch*: escort.

60 *are*: have. *in very happy time*: at just the right moment.

Servant
They would not have you to stir forth today.
Plucking the entrails of an offering forth,
40 They could not find a heart within the beast.
  Caesar
The gods do this in shame of cowardice.
Caesar should be a beast without a heart
If he should stay at home today for fear.
No, Caesar shall not. Danger knows full well
45 That Caesar is more dangerous than he:
We are two lions litter'd in one day,
And I the elder and more terrible.
And Caesar shall go forth.
  Calpurnia
                            Alas, my lord,
Your wisdom is consum'd in confidence.
50 Do not go forth today. Call it my fear
That keeps you in the house, and not your own.
We'll send Mark Antony to the Senate House
And he shall say you are not well today.
Let me, upon my knee, prevail in this.
  Caesar
55 Mark Antony shall say I am not well,
And for thy humour I will stay at home.

Enter Decius

Here's Decius Brutus, he shall tell them so.
  Decius
Caesar, all hail! Good morrow, worthy Caesar,
I come to fetch you to the Senate House.
  Caesar
60 And you are come in very happy time
To bear my greeting to the senators
And tell them that I will not come today.
Cannot is false, and that I dare not, falser:
I will not come today. Tell them so, Decius.
  Calpurnia
65 Say he is sick.

Caesar
Shall Caesar send a lie?
Have I in conquest stretch'd mine arm so far
To be afeard to tell greybeards the truth?
Decius, go tell them Caesar will not come.

Decius
Most mighty Caesar, let me know some cause,
70 Lest I be laugh'd at when I tell them so.

Caesar
The cause is in my will. I will not come:
That is enough to satisfy the Senate.
But for your private satisfaction,
Because I love you, I will let you know:
75 Calpurnia here, my wife, stays me at home.
She dreamt tonight she saw my statue,
Which like a fountain with an hundred spouts
Did run pure blood, and many lusty Romans
Came smiling and did bathe their hands in it.
80 And these does she apply for warnings and portents
And evils imminent, and on her knee
Hath begg'd that I will stay at home today.

Decius
This dream is all amiss interpreted,
It was a vision fair and fortunate.

66 *Have . . . far*: have I made such vast conquests.
67 *afeard*: afraid.
   greybeards: old men.

73 *private*: personal.

76 *statue*: For the regularity of the rhythm, this word must be pronounced with three syllables ('sta-tu-e').
78 *lusty*: vigorous.
80 *apply for*: interpret as.

83 *all amiss*: quite wrongly.
84 *fortunate*: promising good fortune.

88–9 *great men . . . cognizance*: noble men will strive to get their heraldic colours ('tinctures, stains'), souvenirs ('relics'), and badges ('cognizance') to show that they are your servants; in this interpretation, Caesar's blood is merely metaphorical.
91 *expounded*: explained.
92 *when . . . say*: you will be sure I am right when you hear what else I have to say.
93 *know it now*: let me tell you now. *concluded*: finally decided.
96–7 *it were . . . say*: it's very likely that somebody will make a joke of it and say.

85 Your statue spouting blood in many pipes,
In which so many smiling Romans bath'd,
Signifies that from you great Rome shall suck
Reviving blood and that great men shall press
For tinctures, stains, relics, and cognizance.
90 This by Calpurnia's dream is signified.
  Caesar
And this way have you well expounded it.
  Decius
I have, when you have heard what I can say.
And know it now: the Senate have concluded
To give this day a crown to mighty Caesar.
95 If you shall send them word you will not come,
Their minds may change. Besides, it were a mock
Apt to be render'd for someone to say,
'Break up the Senate till another time,
When Caesar's wife shall meet with better dreams.'
100 If Caesar hide himself, shall they not whisper,
'Lo, Caesar is afraid'?
Pardon me, Caesar, for my dear dear love
To your proceeding bids me tell you this,
And reason to my love is liable.
  Caesar
105 How foolish do your fears seem now, Calpurnia!
I am ashamed I did yield to them.
Give me my robe, for I will go.

  Enter Brutus, Ligarius, Metellus, Casca, Trebonius,
  Cinna, *and* Publius

And look where Publius is come to fetch me.
  Publius
Good morrow, Caesar.
  Caesar
                        Welcome, Publius.
110 What, Brutus, are you stirr'd so early too?
Good morrow, Casca. Caius Ligarius,
Caesar was ne'er so much your enemy
As that same ague which hath made you lean.
What is't o'clock?

103 *proceeding*: advancement.
104 *reason . . . liable*: reason gives second place to my love.

106 *ashamed*: ashamèd.

112 *enemy*: Ligarius had fought on Pompey's side in the civil war, but Caesar had pardoned him.
113 *ague*: sickness.
114 *What is't o'clock*: All the characters are very conscious of time.

115 *pains*: trouble.

116 *long a-nights*: late into the night.

121 *in store*: waiting.

128–9 *That . . . upon*: Brutus's heart grieves ('earns') because he knows that being *like* a friend is not the same as really *being* a friend.

Brutus

      Caesar, 'tis strucken eight.

Caesar

115 I thank you for your pains and courtesy.

Enter Antony

See, Antony, that revels long a-nights,
Is notwithstanding up. Good morrow, Antony.

 Antony

So to most noble Caesar.

 Caesar

[*To* Calpurnia]   Bid them prepare within,

           [*Exit* Calpurnia

I am to blame to be thus waited for.

120 Now, Cinna, now, Metellus. What, Trebonius,
I have an hour's talk in store for you.
Remember that you call on me today;
Be near me that I may remember you.

 Trebonius

Caesar, I will. [*Aside*] And so near will I be

125 That your best friends shall wish I had been further.

 Caesar

Good friends, go in and taste some wine with me,
And we, like friends, will straightway go together.

 Brutus

[*Aside*] That every like is not the same, O Caesar,
The heart of Brutus earns to think upon.   [*Exeunt

Act 2 Scene 3
Artemidorus reads the letter he will give to Caesar.

2 *have an eye to*: keep an eye on.
4–5 *There . . . men*: these men all have the same intention.
   bent: directed.
6 *beest*: be.
   look about you: be careful what you do.
7 *security*: over-confidence.
   gives way: makes room for.

9 *Thy lover*: one who loves you.

12 *suitor*: one who makes a request (suit).
14 *Out . . . emulation*: away from the threat of jealous rivalry.
16 *the fates*: the three goddesses who, in classical mythology, controlled man's destiny.
   contrive: conspire.

Act 2 Scene 4
Portia is anxious to know what is happening in the Capitol, and the words of a soothsayer give her more cause for alarm.

1 *I prithee*: I pray you.

4–5 *I would . . . there*: you could have gone there and back again before I could tell you what I really want you to do.
6 *constancy*: firmness, strength of purpose.
7 *Set . . . tongue*: i.e. so she cannot talk about her worries.

SCENE 3

Rome: a street. Enter Artemidorus *reading a paper*

Artemidorus
'Caesar, beware of Brutus, take heed of Cassius, come
not near Casca, have an eye to Cinna, trust not
Trebonius, mark well Metellus Cimber, Decius Brutus
loves thee not, thou hast wronged Caius Ligarius. There
5 is but one mind in all these men, and it is bent against
Caesar. If thou beest not immortal look about you:
security gives way to conspiracy. The mighty gods
defend thee!
                                          Thy lover,
10   Artemidorus.'
Here will I stand till Caesar pass along,
And as a suitor will I give him this.
My heart laments that virtue cannot live
Out of the teeth of emulation.
15 If thou read this, O Caesar, thou mayst live;
If not, the fates with traitors do contrive.   [*Exit*

SCENE 4

Rome: outside Brutus's *house. Enter* Portia *and*
Lucius

Portia
I prithee, boy, run to the Senate House.
Stay not to answer me but get thee gone.
Why dost thou stay?
Lucius
                              To know my errand, madam.
Portia
I would have had thee there and here again
5 Ere I can tell thee what thou shouldst do there.
[*Aside*] O constancy, be strong upon my side,
Set a huge mountain 'tween my heart and tongue!

9 *counsel*: secrets.

10 *yet*: still.

14 *went sickly forth*: was sick when he went out.
take good note: watch carefully.

15 *press*: crowd in on.

18 *bustling rumour*: noise of people rushing about.
fray: fight.

20 *Sooth*: truly.

23 *What . . . o'clock*: what time is it.

25 *stand*: position.

27 *suit*: petition.

29 *To be . . . me*: to be so kind to himself as to listen to me.

I have a man's mind, but a woman's might.
How hard it is for women to keep counsel!—
10 Art thou here yet?

Lucius
            Madam, what should I do?
Run to the Capitol, and nothing else?
And so return to you, and nothing else?

Portia
Yes, bring me word, boy, if thy lord look well,
For he went sickly forth, and take good note
15 What Caesar doth, what suitors press to him.
Hark, boy, what noise is that?

Lucius
I hear none, madam.

Portia
            Prithee listen well:
I heard a bustling rumour, like a fray,
And the wind brings it from the Capitol.

Lucius
20 Sooth, madam, I hear nothing.

Enter the Soothsayer

Portia
Come hither, fellow, which way hast thou been?

Soothsayer
At mine own house, good lady.

Portia
What is't o'clock?

Soothsayer
            About the ninth hour, lady.

Portia
Is Caesar yet gone to the Capitol?

Soothsayer
25 Madam, not yet. I go to take my stand
To see him pass on to the Capitol.

Portia
Thou hast some suit to Caesar, hast thou not?

Soothsayer
That I have, lady, if it will please Caesar
To be so good to Caesar as to hear me:
30 I shall beseech him to befriend himself.

31 *any harm's*: that any harm is.

32 *chance*: happen.

35 *praetors*: administrators of justice.

37 *void*: clear, empty.

41 *speed*: favour.
42–3 *Brutus . . . grant*: Portia invents an
   explanation for her anxiety in case
   Lucius did overhear her.
44 *commend me*: give my kind regards.
45 *merry*: cheerful.
46s.d. *severally*: in different directions, at
   separate doors.

Portia
Why, know'st thou any harm's intended towards him?
   Soothsayer
None that I know will be, much that I fear may chance.
Good morrow to you. Here the street is narrow:
The throng that follows Caesar at the heels,
35 Of senators, of praetors, common suitors,
Will crowd a feeble man almost to death.
I'll get me to a place more void, and there
Speak to great Caesar as he comes along.   [*Exit*
   Portia
I must go in. [*Aside*] Ay me, how weak a thing
40 The heart of woman is! O Brutus,
The heavens speed thee in thine enterprise!
Sure the boy heard me. Brutus hath a suit
That Caesar will not grant. O, I grow faint.—
Run, Lucius, and commend me to my lord,
45 Say I am merry. Come to me again
And bring me word what he doth say to thee.

[*Exeunt severally*

ACT 3

Act 3 Scene 1
Caesar's refusal to grant a petition is the
cue for the conspirators to stab him. Brutus
takes charge of the situation, and agrees
that Antony shall speak at Caesar's funeral.
Alone on the stage, Antony prophesies civil
war—and sends a message to Octavius.

0s.d. *Lepidus*: Plutarch mentions
    Lepidus's presence on this occasion—
    although Shakespeare gives the
    character no lines to speak.

3 *schedule*: document.

4 *o'er-read*: read through.
5 *your best leisure*: when it is most
    convenient for you.

7 *touches Caesar nearer*: more closely
    concerns yourself.

8 *serv'd*: dealt with.

10 *Sirrah*: fellow.
    place: way.

SCENE 1

Rome: the Capitol. Flourish. Enter Caesar, Brutus,
Cassius, Casca, Decius, Metellus, Trebonius, Cinna,
Antony, Lepidus, Artemidorus, Publius, Popillius,
Ligarius, *and the* Soothsayer

Caesar
The Ides of March are come.
  Soothsayer
Ay, Caesar, but not gone.
  Artemidorus
Hail, Caesar! Read this schedule.
  Decius
Trebonius doth desire you to o'er-read
5 (At your best leisure) this his humble suit.
  Artemidorus
O Caesar, read mine first, for mine's a suit
That touches Caesar nearer. Read it, great Caesar.
  Caesar
What touches us ourself shall be last serv'd.
  Artemidorus
Delay not, Caesar, read it instantly.
  Caesar
10 What, is the fellow mad?
  Publius
                    Sirrah, give place.
  Cassius
What, urge you your petitions in the street?
Come to the Capitol.

Caesar enters the Capitol, the rest following

Popillius
I wish your enterprise today may thrive.

Cassius
What enterprise, Popillius?
Popillius
                                    Fare you well.

Leaves him and joins Caesar

Brutus
15 What said Popillius Lena?
        Cassius
He wish'd today our enterprise might thrive.
I fear our purpose is discovered.
        Brutus
Look how he makes to Caesar, mark him.
        Cassius
Casca, be sudden, for we fear prevention.
20 Brutus, what shall be done? If this be known
Cassius or Caesar never shall turn back,
For I will slay myself.
        Brutus
                                    Cassius, be constant.
Popillius Lena speaks not of our purposes,
For look he smiles, and Caesar doth not change.
        Cassius
25 Trebonius knows his time, for look you, Brutus,
He draws Mark Antony out of the way.
                        [*Exeunt* Antony *and* Trebonius
        Decius
Where is Metellus Cimber? Let him go
And presently prefer his suit to Caesar.
        Brutus
He is address'd, press near and second him.
        Cinna
30 Casca, you are the first that rears your hand.
        Caesar
Are we all ready? What is now amiss
That Caesar and his Senate must redress?
        Metellus
Most high, most mighty, and most puissant Caesar,
Metellus Cimber throws before thy seat
35 An humble heart.

17 *discovered*: discoverèd.

18 *makes to*: proceeds towards.

19 *sudden*: quick of action.
we fear prevention: we're afraid they're going to stop us.
21 *Cassius or Caesar*: either Cassius or Caesar.

22 *constant*: firm, resolute.

25 *knows his time*: knows when to act.

28 *presently*: immediately.
prefer: present.

29 *address'd*: ready.
press near: crowd around.
second: support.
30 *rears*: raises.

31 *amiss*: wrong.

32 *redress*: correct.

33 *puissant*: powerful.

35 *prevent*: forestall.

36 *These . . . courtesies*: this bowing and curtsying in humility.
37 *blood*: spirit.
38–9 *turn . . . children*: make the first preordained laws of the universe seem like the rules of a children's game.
38 *first decree*: that which has been decreed from the beginning of time.
39–42 *Be not . . . fools*: don't be foolish ('fond') and think that Caesar's spirit ('blood') can be so false to its real nature ('true quality') as to be softened by the sort of thing that works with fools.
43 *Low-crooked curtsies*: crookèd; knees bending down.
base spaniel fawning: cringing like a spaniel (a dog that Shakespeare particularly associates with servile behaviour).
44 *decree*: law.
banished: banishèd.
46 *spurn*: kick.
47 *doth not wrong*: does not act unjustly.
47–8 *nor . . . satisfied*: and without good reason ('cause') he will not be convinced—i.e. that this sentence should be repealed.
51 *repealing*: recalling from exile.
54 *freedom of repeal*: permission to be recalled from exile.

57 *enfranchisement*: restoration of citizenship.
58 *I could . . . you*: if I were like you, I would easily be persuaded.
59 *pray to move*: entreat others to change their minds.
60 *the northern star*: the pole star, which sailors use for steering their course.
61 *resting*: permanent.
62 *no fellow*: nothing like it.
firmament: heavens.
63 *unnumber'd*: innumerable.
65 *but one*: only one.
hold his place: keeps still in the same position.
66 *furnish'd*: stocked.
67 *apprehensive*: capable of understanding.

Caesar

      I must prevent thee, Cimber.
These couchings and these lowly courtesies
Might fire the blood of ordinary men
And turn preordinance and first decree
Into the law of children. Be not fond
40 To think that Caesar bears such rebel blood
That will be thaw'd from the true quality
With that which melteth fools—I mean sweet words,
Low-crooked curtsies, and base spaniel fawning.
Thy brother by decree is banished:
45 If thou dost bend, and pray, and fawn for him,
I spurn thee like a cur out of my way.
Know Caesar doth not wrong, nor without cause
Will he be satisfied.

 Metellus
Is there no voice more worthy than my own
50 To sound more sweetly in great Caesar's ear
For the repealing of my banish'd brother?

 Brutus
I kiss thy hand, but not in flattery, Caesar,
Desiring thee that Publius Cimber may
Have an immediate freedom of repeal.

 Caesar
55 What, Brutus?

 Cassius
      Pardon, Caesar! Caesar, pardon!
As low as to thy foot doth Cassius fall
To beg enfranchisement for Publius Cimber.

 Caesar
I could be well mov'd, if I were as you;
If I could pray to move, prayers would move me.
60 But I am constant as the northern star,
Of whose true-fix'd and resting quality
There is no fellow in the firmament.
The skies are painted with unnumber'd sparks,
They are all fire, and every one doth shine;
65 But there's but one in all doth hold his place.
So in the world: 'tis furnish'd well with men,
And men are flesh and blood, and apprehensive;
Yet in the number I do know but one

69 *unassailable*: constant, resolutely.
   holds . . . rank: keeps in the same
   position.
70 *Unshak'd of motion*: undisturbed by
   the movements of objects outside
   himself.

That unassailable holds on his rank,
70 Unshak'd of motion, and that I am he
Let me a little show it, even in this:
That I was constant Cimber should be banish'd,
And constant do remain to keep him so.

Cinna
O Caesar—

Caesar
     Hence! Wilt thou lift up Olympus?

74 *Olympus*: a mountain in Greece, said
   to be the home of the gods.

Decius
75 Great Caesar—

Caesar
      Doth not Brutus bootless kneel?

75 *bootless*: without success (the
   implication is that no one can
   succeed where Brutus fails).

Casca
Speak hands for me!

   They stab Caesar

Caesar
Et tu, Brute?—Then fall, Caesar!   [*Dies*

77 *Et tu, Brute*: and you, Brutus; '*Brute*'
   (in the Latin vocative case) has two
   syllables.

Cinna
Liberty! Freedom! Tyranny is dead!
Run hence, proclaim, cry it about the streets.

Cassius
80 Some to the common pulpits, and cry out,
'Liberty, freedom, and enfranchisement!'

80 *common pulpits*: public platforms.
81 *enfranchisement*: citizenship.

Brutus
People and senators, be not affrighted,
Fly not, stand still! Ambition's debt is paid.

82 *affrighted*: afraid.
83 *Ambition's . . . paid*: ambition has got
   what it deserved.

Casca
Go to the pulpit, Brutus.

Decius
      And Cassius too.

Brutus
85 Where's Publius?

85 *Publius*: an aged senator, too weak to
   run away.

Cinna
Here, quite confounded with this mutiny.

86 *mutiny*: discord.

Metellus
Stand fast together lest some friend of Caesar's
Should chance—

87 *fast*: close.
88 *chance*: happen.

'Et tu, Brute?', (3, 1, 77). David Waller as Caesar and Roger Allam as Brutus, Royal Shakespeare Company, 1988.

89 *Talk . . . standing*: there's no need to think of defending ourselves. *good cheer*: don't worry.

93 *do . . . mischief*: harm you because you are old.

94 *abide*: face the consequences.

96 *amaz'd*: stupefied.
97 *wives*: women.
98 *As it*: as if it.
doomsday: the Day of Judgement.
Fates. . . pleasures: we will attend the wishes of the goddesses of destiny.
99–100 *That . . . upon*: We know that we shall all die; people only worry about when they will die, and how long they will live.
100 *stand upon*: argue about.

103 *Grant that*: if you agree to that.
104 *abridg'd*: shortened.

108 *market-place*: the Forum.

111 *wash*: immerse (hands and swords).
112 *lofty scene*: noble action.
113 *unborn*: not yet founded.
accents: languages.

Brutus
Talk not of standing. Publius, good cheer,
90 There is no harm intended to your person,
Nor to no Roman else. So tell them, Publius.
Cassius
And leave us, Publius, lest that the people,
Rushing on us, should do your age some mischief.
Brutus
Do so, and let no man abide this deed
95 But we the doers.   [*Exeunt all but the conspirators*

Enter Trebonius

Cassius
Where is Antony?
Trebonius
                              Fled to his house amaz'd.
Men, wives, and children stare, cry out, and run
As it were doomsday.
Brutus
                              Fates, we will know your pleasures.
That we shall die we know: 'tis but the time,
100 And drawing days out, that men stand upon.
Casca
Why, he that cuts off twenty years of life
Cuts off so many years of fearing death.
Brutus
Grant that, and then is death a benefit.
So are we Caesar's friends, that have abridg'd
105 His time of fearing death. Stoop, Romans, stoop,
And let us bathe our hands in Caesar's blood
Up to the elbows and besmear our swords.
Then walk we forth, even to the market-place,
And waving our red weapons o'er our heads
110 Let's all cry, 'Peace, freedom, and liberty!'
Cassius
Stoop then and wash. How many ages hence
Shall this our lofty scene be acted over
In states unborn and accents yet unknown!

Brutus
How many times shall Caesar bleed in sport,
115 That now on Pompey's basis lies along
No worthier than the dust!
Cassius
                   So oft as that shall be,
So often shall the knot of us be call'd
The men that gave their country liberty.
Decius
What, shall we forth?
Cassius
               Ay, every man away.
120 Brutus shall lead, and we will grace his heels
With the most boldest and best hearts of Rome.

Enter a Servant

Brutus
Soft, who comes here? A friend of Antony's.
Servant
Thus, Brutus, did my master bid me kneel,
Thus did Mark Antony bid me fall down,
125 And, being prostrate, thus he bade me say:
Brutus is noble, wise, valiant, and honest;
Caesar was mighty, bold, royal, and loving.
Say I love Brutus, and I honour him;
Say I fear'd Caesar, honour'd him, and lov'd him.
130 If Brutus will vouchsafe that Antony
May safely come to him and be resolv'd
How Caesar hath deserv'd to lie in death,
Mark Antony shall not love Caesar dead
So well as Brutus living, but will follow
135 The fortunes and affairs of noble Brutus
Through the hazards of this untrod state
With all true faith. So says my master Antony.
Brutus
Thy master is a wise and valiant Roman,
I never thought him worse.
140 Tell him, so please him come unto this place,
He shall be satisfied and by my honour
Depart untouch'd.

---

114 *in sport*: for entertainment.
115 *Pompey's basis*: the pedestal of Pompey's statue.
along: stretched out.
116 *oft*: often.
117 *knot*: band.
119 *shall we forth*: shall we go out.
120 *grace his heels*: honour him by following on his heels.
122 *Soft*: wait.
126 *honest*: honourable; these two words develop a wide range of meanings during the course of the play.
127 *royal*: noble.
130 *vouchsafe*: allow.
131 *resolv'd*: satisfied.
136 *untrod state*: unfamiliar state of affairs.
140 *so please him*: if he will.

142 *presently*: at once.
143 *well to friend*: as a good friend.
145–6 *my . . . purpose*: my suspicions usually prove to be uncomfortably accurate.
149 *spoils*: trophies.
150 *this little measure*: the ground his body lies on.

152 *let blood*: killed; blood-letting was common surgical procedure to reduce fever.
rank: overgrown; excessively swollen; of equal status.
155 *Of . . . as*: half as worthy as.
157 *bear me hard*: have any grudge against me.
158 *purpled*: crimson with blood.
reek: steam.
159 *Fulfil*: carry out.
Live: if I live.
160 *apt*: ready.
161 *mean*: means.
163 *choice*: best.
master: most powerful.
164 *beg . . . us*: do not ask us to kill you.

169 *pitiful*: full of pity.
170 *pity . . . Rome*: pity for the general injustice suffered by Rome.
171 *As fire . . . pity*: just as one fire drives out another, so pity (for Rome) destroys pity (for Caesar).
172 *For your part*: as far as you are concerned.

Servant
                   I'll fetch him presently.

                              [*Exit* Servant

Brutus
I know that we shall have him well to friend.
    Cassius
I wish we may. But yet have I a mind
145 That fears him much, and my misgiving still
Falls shrewdly to the purpose.

Enter Antony

Brutus
But here comes Antony. Welcome, Mark Antony!
    Antony
O mighty Caesar! Dost thou lie so low?
Are all thy conquests, glories, triumphs, spoils
150 Shrunk to this little measure? Fare thee well!
I know not, gentlemen, what you intend,
Who else must be let blood, who else is rank.
If I myself, there is no hour so fit
As Caesar's death's hour, nor no instrument
155 Of half that worth as those your swords made rich
With the most noble blood of all this world.
I do beseech ye, if you bear me hard,
Now, whilst your purpled hands do reek and smoke,
Fulfil your pleasure. Live a thousand years,
160 I shall not find myself so apt to die:
No place will please me so, no mean of death,
As here by Caesar, and by you cut off,
The choice and master spirits of this age.
    Brutus
O Antony, beg not your death of us.
165 Though now we must appear bloody and cruel,
As by our hands and this our present act
You see we do, yet see you but our hands
And this the bleeding business they have done.
Our hearts you see not, they are pitiful;
170 And pity to the general wrong of Rome—
As fire drives out fire, so pity pity—
Hath done this deed on Caesar. For your part,

173 *leaden points*: i.e. are harmless.

174–5 *Our arms . . . in*: our arms, which have the power to harm, and our hearts, with the affection ('temper') of brothers, welcome you as one of us.

176 *reverence*: respect.

177 *voice*: vote, opinion.

178 *disposing*: distribution.
dignities: offices and awards.

181 *deliver . . . cause*: explain the reason to you.

183 *proceeded*: acted.

191 *credit*: reputation.
192 *conceit*: imagine.
196 *dearer*: more keenly.
199 *corse*: corpse.
202 *close*: come to an agreement.
204 *bay'd*: driven (like a hunted stag) to a standstill.
hart: deer; with an obvious pun on 'heart'.

206 *Sign'd*: marked.
spoil: slaughter; the capture of the quarry and division of rewards in stag-hunting.
Lethe: i.e. life-blood; Lethe was the river in Hades whose waters brought everlasting forgetfulness of the past.

207–8 *O world . . . thee*: the whole world was Caesar's territory, and Caesar was the life-force of the world; Antony extends his pun.

To you our swords have leaden points, Mark Antony;
Our arms in strength of malice, and our hearts
175 Of brothers' temper, do receive you in
With all kind love, good thoughts, and reverence.
    Cassius
Your voice shall be as strong as any man's
In the disposing of new dignities.
    Brutus
Only be patient till we have appeas'd
180 The multitude, beside themselves with fear,
And then we will deliver you the cause
Why I, that did love Caesar when I struck him,
Have thus proceeded.
    Antony
                    I doubt not of your wisdom.
Let each man render me his bloody hand.
185 First, Marcus Brutus, will I shake with you;
Next, Caius Cassius, do I take your hand;
Now, Decius Brutus, yours; now yours, Metellus;
Yours, Cinna; and, my valiant Casca, yours;
Though last, not least in love, yours, good Trebonius.
190 Gentlemen all—alas, what shall I say?
My credit now stands on such slippery ground
That one of two bad ways you must conceit me,
Either a coward or a flatterer.
That I did love thee, Caesar, O, 'tis true.
195 If then thy spirit look upon us now,
Shall it not grieve thee dearer than thy death
To see thy Antony making his peace,
Shaking the bloody fingers of thy foes—
Most noble—in the presence of thy corse?
200 Had I as many eyes as thou hast wounds,
Weeping as fast as they stream forth thy blood,
It would become me better than to close
In terms of friendship with thine enemies.
Pardon me, Julius! Here wast thou bay'd, brave hart,
205 Here didst thou fall, and here thy hunters stand,
Sign'd in thy spoil and crimson'd in thy Lethe.
O world! Thou wast the forest to this hart,
And this indeed, O world, the heart of thee.
How like a deer strucken by many princes
210 Dost thou here lie!

Cassius
Mark Antony—
    Antony
                Pardon me, Caius Cassius,
The enemies of Caesar shall say this;
Then, in a friend, it is cold modesty.
    Cassius
I blame you not for praising Caesar so,

215 But what compact mean you to have with us?
Will you be prick'd in number of our friends,
Or shall we on and not depend on you?
    Antony
Therefore I took your hands, but was indeed
Sway'd from the point by looking down on Caesar.

220 Friends am I with you all, and love you all,
Upon this hope, that you shall give me reasons
Why and wherein Caesar was dangerous.
    Brutus
Or else were this a savage spectacle.
Our reasons are so full of good regard

225 That were you, Antony, the son of Caesar
You should be satisfied.
    Antony
                That's all I seek,
And am, moreover, suitor that I may
Produce his body to the market-place,
And in the pulpit, as becomes a friend,

230 Speak in the order of his funeral.
    Brutus
You shall, Mark Antony.
    Cassius
               Brutus, a word with you.
[*Aside to* Brutus] You know not what you do. Do not consent
That Antony speak in his funeral.
Know you how much the people may be mov'd

235 By that which he will utter?
    Brutus
[*Aside to* Cassius]   By your pardon,
I will myself into the pulpit first
And show the reason of our Caesar's death.

---

213 *modesty*: understatement.

215 *compact*: agreement.
216 *prick'd*: marked (by making a prick, or dot, on the list).
217 *on*: continue.

218 *Therefore*: for that reason (i.e. to indicate that I am one of you).
219 *Sway'd*: diverted.

221 *Upon this hope*: with the hope that.
222 *wherein*: in what way.

223 *else*: otherwise.
224 *good regard*: serious consideration.

227 *And . . . suitor*: and as well as this I have a request.
228 *Produce*: bring out.

230 *order*: ceremony.

236 *will*: will go.

238 *What . . . speak*: whatever Antony may say.
protest: declare.

242 *advantage*: benefit.

243 *fall*: happen.

246 *devise of*: think of about.

257 *lived*: livèd.
tide of times: stream of history.
258 *costly*: precious.

260 *ope*: open.

262 *light*: fall.
263 *Domestic*: within the state.
264: *cumber*: overwhelm.

265 *in use*: usual.

267 *but smile*: only smile.
268 *quarter'd*: cut to pieces.
269 *All . . . deeds*: the familiarity of cruel deeds will smother all pity.
270 *ranging*: hunting.
271 *Ate*: The goddess of revenge; the name has two syllables.

What Antony shall speak, I will protest
He speaks by leave and by permission,
240 And that we are contented Caesar shall
Have all true rites and lawful ceremonies.
It shall advantage more than do us wrong.
        Cassius
[*Aside to* Brutus] I know not what may fall, I like it not.
        Brutus
Mark Antony, here take you Caesar's body.
245 You shall not in your funeral speech blame us,
But speak all good you can devise of Caesar
And say you do't by our permission,
Else shall you not have any hand at all
About his funeral. And you shall speak
250 In the same pulpit whereto I am going,
After my speech is ended.
        Antony
                                Be it so,
I do desire no more.
        Brutus
Prepare the body then and follow us.
                                [*Exeunt all but* Antony
        Antony
O, pardon me, thou bleeding piece of earth,
255 That I am meek and gentle with these butchers!
Thou art the ruins of the noblest man
That ever lived in the tide of times.
Woe to the hand that shed this costly blood!
Over thy wounds now do I prophesy—
260 Which like dumb mouths do ope their ruby lips
To beg the voice and utterance of my tongue—
A curse shall light upon the limbs of men:
Domestic fury and fierce civil strife
Shall cumber all the parts of Italy;
265 Blood and destruction shall be so in use
And dreadful objects so familiar
That mothers shall but smile when they behold
Their infants quarter'd with the hands of war,
All pity chok'd with custom of fell deeds;
270 And Caesar's spirit, ranging for revenge,
With Ate by his side come hot from hell,

272 *confines*: regions.
273 *Cry havoc*: Only a king could give this order, which was the signal for mass slaughter and plunder.
275 *carrion*: dead.

276s.d. *Enter . . . Servant*: This is the pivotal moment of the play: as Antony's rhetoric reaches its highest point, he is brought down to earth with the appearance of the Servant— whose assistance is necessary for the dignified removal of Caesar's body.

282 *big*: swollen with grief.
283 *Passion*: emotion.
284 *beads of sorrow*: tears.

286 *lies*: is in camp.
     seven leagues: about twenty-one miles.
287 *Post*: ride fast.
     chanc'd: happened.

290 *Hie*: hurry.
291 *not back*: not go back.
     corse: corpse.
292 *try*: test.
293 *take*: react to.
294 *cruel issue*: results of the cruelty.
295 *According . . . which*: depending on which (i.e. the citizens' reactions).
     discourse: describe.

Shall in these confines with a monarch's voice
Cry havoc and let slip the dogs of war,
That this foul deed shall smell above the earth
275 With carrion men groaning for burial.

Enter Octavius's *Servant*

You serve Octavius Caesar, do you not?
   Servant
I do, Mark Antony.
   Antony
Caesar did write for him to come to Rome.
   Servant
He did receive his letters, and is coming,
280 And bid me say to you by word of mouth—

Seeing the body

O Caesar!
   Antony
Thy heart is big, get thee apart and weep.
Passion, I see, is catching, for mine eyes,
Seeing those beads of sorrow stand in thine,
285 Began to water. Is thy master coming?
   Servant
He lies tonight within seven leagues of Rome.
   Antony
Post back with speed and tell him what hath chanc'd.
Here is a mourning Rome, a dangerous Rome,
No Rome of safety for Octavius yet:
290 Hie hence and tell him so. Yet stay awhile,
Thou shalt not back till I have borne this corse
Into the market-place. There shall I try
In my oration how the people take
The cruel issue of these bloody men,
295 According to the which thou shalt discourse
To young Octavius of the state of things.
Lend me your hand.   [*Exeunt with* Caesar's *body*

'You all do know this mantle', (*3*, 2, 168). David Schofield as Mark Antony, Royal Shakespeare Company, 1983.

Act 3 Scene 2
Brutus gives reasons to the citizens, but
Antony moves their hearts to mutiny with
his oration at Caesar's funeral. Octavius has
entered the city.

0s.d. *Plebeians*: commoners.

1 *satisfied*: given a satisfactory
explanation.

2 *give me audience*: listen to me.

4 *part the numbers*: divide the crowd.

7 *public*: concerning the public; spoken
in public.
rendered: renderèd.

10 *severally*: separately.
rendered: renderèd.

12 *till the last*: until the end.
13–33 *Romans . . . reply*: Brutus tries to
present a reasoned argument—in
prose.
14–16 *Believe me . . . believe*: believe
me because I am a man of honour,
and remember that I am an
honourable man whom you can
believe.
16 *Censure*: judge (not necessarily in a
negative sense).
17 *senses*: understanding.

22 *Had you*: would you.

25 *fortunate*: successful (in war).

SCENE 2

Rome: the Forum. Enter Brutus *and* Cassius *with the*
Plebeians

All
We will be satisfied! Let us be satisfied!
Brutus
Then follow me and give me audience, friends.
Cassius, go you into the other street
And part the numbers.
5 Those that will hear me speak, let 'em stay here;
Those that will follow Cassius, go with him;
And public reasons shall be rendered
Of Caesar's death.
First Plebeian
                    I will hear Brutus speak.
Second Plebeian
I will hear Cassius and compare their reasons
10 When severally we hear them rendered.
                    [*Exit* Cassius *with some of the* Plebeians

Brutus *goes into the pulpit*

Third Plebeian
The noble Brutus is ascended, silence!
Brutus
Be patient till the last.
Romans, countrymen, and lovers, hear me for my
cause, and be silent that you may hear. Believe me for
15 mine honour, and have respect to mine honour that you
may believe. Censure me in your wisdom, and awake
your senses that you may the better judge. If there be
any in this assembly, any dear friend of Caesar's, to him
I say that Brutus' love to Caesar was no less than his. If
20 then that friend demand why Brutus rose against
Caesar, this is my answer: not that I loved Caesar less,
but that I loved Rome more. Had you rather Caesar
were living, and die all slaves, than that Caesar were
dead, to live all freemen? As Caesar loved me, I weep for
25 him; as he was fortunate, I rejoice at it; as he was valiant,

29 *would be*: would wish to be.

30 *rude*: uncivilized.

36 *do to Brutus*: i.e. if Brutus becomes a
tyrant.
question of: reasons for.
37 *enrolled*: recorded upon a roll or
parchment.
extenuated: belittled.
38 *enforced*: emphasized.

41 *no hand in*: was not responsible for.
42 *a place in the commonwealth*: the
right to live in a free republic.

44 *lover*: friend.

50 *parts*: qualities.

I honour him; but, as he was ambitious, I slew him.
There is tears for his love, joy for his fortune, honour for
his valour, and death for his ambition. Who is here so
base that would be a bondman? If any, speak, for him
30 have I offended. Who is here so rude that would not be
a Roman? If any, speak, for him have I offended. Who is
here so vile that will not love his country? If any, speak,
for him have I offended. I pause for a reply.

All
None, Brutus, none.
Brutus
35 Then none have I offended. I have done no more to
Caesar than you shall do to Brutus. The question of his
death is enrolled in the Capitol, his glory not extenuated
wherein he was worthy nor his offences enforced for
which he suffered death.

Enter Mark Antony *and others with* Caesar's *body*

40 Here comes his body, mourned by Mark Antony, who,
though he had no hand in his death, shall receive the
benefit of his dying, a place in the commonwealth, as
which of you shall not? With this I depart: that, as I slew
my best lover for the good of Rome, I have the same
45 dagger for myself when it shall please my country to
need my death.

Comes down

All
Live, Brutus, live, live!
First Plebeian
Bring him with triumph home unto his house.
Second Plebeian
Give him a statue with his ancestors.
Third Plebeian
50 Let him be Caesar.
Fourth Plebeian   Caesar's better parts
Shall be crown'd in Brutus.

First Plebeian

                                        We'll bring him to his house
With shouts and clamours.
Brutus

                                                My countrymen—
Second Plebeian
Peace, silence, Brutus speaks!
First Plebeian

                                            Peace ho!
Brutus
Good countrymen, let me depart alone,
55 And, for my sake, stay here with Antony.
Do grace to Caesar's corpse, and grace his speech
Tending to Caesar's glories, which Mark Antony
(By our permission) is allow'd to make.
I do entreat you, not a man depart,
60 Save I alone, till Antony have spoke.   [*Exit*
First Plebeian
Stay ho, and let us hear Mark Antony.
Third Plebeian
Let him go up into the public chair,
We'll hear him. Noble Antony, go up.
Antony
For Brutus' sake, I am beholding to you.

Goes into the pulpit

Fourth Plebeian
65 What does he say of Brutus?
Third Plebeian

                                        He says for Brutus' sake
He finds himself beholding to us all.
Fourth Plebeian
'Twere best he speak no harm of Brutus here!
First Plebeian
This Caesar was a tyrant.
Third Plebeian
                                        Nay, that's certain:
We are blest that Rome is rid of him.
Second Plebeian
70 Peace, let us hear what Antony can say.

56 *Do grace*: honour.
   and grace: and respect.
57 *Tending to*: referring to.

62 *public chair*: orator's platform.

64 *For Brutus' . . . you*: I am indebted to
   you, thanks to Brutus.

Antony
You gentle Romans—
All
                Peace ho, let us hear him.
Antony
Friends, Romans, countrymen, lend me your ears!
I come to bury Caesar, not to praise him.
The evil that men do lives after them,
75 The good is oft interred with their bones:
So let it be with Caesar. The noble Brutus
Hath told you Caesar was ambitious;
If it were so, it was a grievous fault,
And grievously hath Caesar answer'd it.
80 Here, under leave of Brutus and the rest—
For Brutus is an honourable man,
So are they all, all honourable men—
Come I to speak in Caesar's funeral.
He was my friend, faithful and just to me,
85 But Brutus says he was ambitious,
And Brutus is an honourable man.
He hath brought many captives home to Rome,
Whose ransoms did the general coffers fill;
Did this in Caesar seem ambitious?
90 When that the poor have cried, Caesar hath wept:
Ambition should be made of sterner stuff;
Yet Brutus says he was ambitious,
And Brutus is an honourable man.
You all did see that on the Lupercal
95 I thrice presented him a kingly crown,
Which he did thrice refuse. Was this ambition?
Yet Brutus says he was ambitious,
And sure he is an honourable man.
I speak not to disprove what Brutus spoke,
100 But here I am to speak what I do know.
You all did love him once, not without cause;
What cause withholds you then to mourn for him?
O judgement, thou art fled to brutish beasts,
And men have lost their reason! Bear with me,
105 My heart is in the coffin there with Caesar,
And I must pause till it come back to me.

72–249 *Friends . . . another*: Antony uses the skills of rhetoric and the power of verse to sway the emotions of the citizens; See 'Shakespeare's Plutarch', p.107.
72 *lend . . . ears*: listen to me.
75 *interred*: interrèd: buried—i.e. forgotten.
80 *under leave of*: with permission from.
88 *general coffers*: public treasury.
91 *sterner*: stronger.
94 *on the Lupercal*: on the feast of Lupercal (see note on *1*, 1, 69).
99 *disprove*: contradict.
102 *withholds*: prevents.
103 *brutish*: Antony seems to be making a pun on Brutus's name and the Latin word *brutus* (= dull, without reason).

First Plebeian
Methinks there is much reason in his sayings.
Second Plebeian
If thou consider rightly of the matter,
Caesar has had great wrong.
Third Plebeian
                                          Has he, masters!
110 I fear there will a worse come in his place.
Fourth Plebeian
Mark'd ye his words? He would not take the crown,
Therefore 'tis certain he was not ambitious.
First Plebeian
If it be found so, some will dear abide it.
Second Plebeian
Poor soul, his eyes are red as fire with weeping.
Third Plebeian
115 There's not a nobler man in Rome than Antony.
Fourth Plebeian
Now mark him, he begins again to speak.
Antony
But yesterday the word of Caesar might
Have stood against the world; now lies he there,
And none so poor to do him reverence.
120 O masters, if I were dispos'd to stir
Your hearts and minds to mutiny and rage,
I should do Brutus wrong and Cassius wrong,
Who (you all know) are honourable men.
I will not do them wrong; I rather choose
125 To wrong the dead, to wrong myself and you,
Than I will wrong such honourable men.
But here's a parchment with the seal of Caesar,
I found it in his closet, 'tis his will.
Let but the commons hear this testament—
130 Which, pardon me, I do not mean to read—
And they would go and kiss dead Caesar's wounds
And dip their napkins in his sacred blood,
Yea, beg a hair of him for memory,
And, dying, mention it within their wills,
135 Bequeathing it as a rich legacy
Unto their issue.

109 *Has he, masters!*: he has indeed, masters!

111 *Mark'd . . . words*: did you hear what he said.

113 *be found*: can be proved.
dear abide it: pay dearly for it.

116 *mark*: listen to.

117 *But*: only.
118 *stood against*: overcome the opposition of.
119 *none . . . reverence*: nobody has the humility to show respect.
120 *dispos'd*: inclined.

125 *wrong the dead*: i.e. by not defending Caesar from being called ambitious.
wrong myself: i.e. by not speaking what I know to be true.
and you: i.e. by allowing you to be deceived by Brutus.
127 *parchment*: document.
128 *closet*: study.
129 *commons*: citizens.
testament: will.
132 *napkins*: handkerchiefs.

136 *issue*: children.

Fourth Plebeian
We'll hear the will. Read it, Mark Antony.
    All
The will, the will, we will hear Caesar's will!
    Antony
Have patience, gentle friends, I must not read it.

140 *meet*: fitting.

140 It is not meet you know how Caesar lov'd you:
You are not wood, you are not stones, but men,
And, being men, hearing the will of Caesar,
It will inflame you, it will make you mad.
'Tis good you know not that you are his heirs,
145 For if you should, O, what would come of it?
    Fourth Plebeian
Read the will, we'll hear it, Antony.
You shall read us the will, Caesar's will!
    Antony
Will you be patient? Will you stay awhile?

149 *o'ershot myself*: gone too far.

I have o'ershot myself to tell you of it.
150 I fear I wrong the honourable men
Whose daggers have stabb'd Caesar, I do fear it.
    Fourth Plebeian
They were traitors. Honourable men!
    All
The will! The testament!
    Second Plebeian
They were villains, murderers! The will, read the will!
    Antony
155 You will compel me then to read the will?
Then make a ring about the corpse of Caesar
And let me show you him that made the will.
Shall I descend? And will you give me leave?
    All
Come down.
    Second Plebeian
160 Descend.
    Third Plebeian
You shall have leave.

Antony comes down from the pulpit

Fourth Plebeian
A ring, stand round.
First Plebeian
Stand from the hearse, stand from the body.
Second Plebeian
Room for Antony, most noble Antony.
Antony
165 Nay, press not so upon me, stand far off.
All
Stand back! Room, bear back!
Antony
If you have tears, prepare to shed them now.
You all do know this mantle. I remember
The first time ever Caesar put it on,
170 'Twas on a summer's evening, in his tent,
That day he overcame the Nervii.
Look, in this place ran Cassius' dagger through;
See what a rent the envious Casca made;
Through this the well-beloved Brutus stabb'd,
175 And as he pluck'd his cursed steel away,
Mark how the blood of Caesar follow'd it,
As rushing out of doors to be resolv'd
If Brutus so unkindly knock'd or no,
For Brutus, as you know, was Caesar's angel.
180 Judge, O you gods, how dearly Caesar lov'd him!
This was the most unkindest cut of all.
For when the noble Caesar saw him stab,
Ingratitude, more strong than traitors' arms,
Quite vanquish'd him. Then burst his mighty heart,
185 And, in his mantle muffling up his face,
Even at the base of Pompey's statue
(Which all the while ran blood) great Caesar fell.
O, what a fall was there, my countrymen!
Then I, and you, and all of us fell down,
190 Whilst bloody treason flourish'd over us.
O, now you weep, and I perceive you feel
The dint of pity. These are gracious drops.
Kind souls, what weep you when you but behold
Our Caesar's vesture wounded? Look you here,
195 Here is himself, marr'd as you see with traitors.

165 *far*: further.

168 *mantle*: cloak.

171 *Nervii*: the most warlike of all the Gallic tribes, conquered by Caesar in 57 BC.
173 *envious*: malicious.
174 *well-beloved*: well-belovèd.
175 *cursed*: cursèd.

177 *resolv'd*: convinced.
178 *unkindly*: unnaturally; cruelly.

181 *most unkindest cut*: the most cruel wound; the double superlative is used for emphasis.

184 *Then . . . heart*: Antony implies that the sight of Brutus amongst the conspirators was the real cause of Caesar's death.
186 *statue*: The final e must be pronounced (see *2, 2, 76* note).
187 *Which . . . blood*: which was streaming with [Caesar's] blood all the time.
190 *flourish'd*: thrived; triumphed.

192 *dint*: blow.
gracious: honourable.
193 *but*: only.
194 *vesture*: clothing.
195 *marr'd*: mutilated.

First Plebeian

O piteous spectacle!

Second Plebeian

O noble Caesar!

Third Plebeian

O woeful day!

Fourth Plebeian

O traitors, villains!

First Plebeian

200 O most bloody sight!

Second Plebeian

We will be reveng'd!

All

Revenge! About! Seek! Burn! Fire! Kill!

Slay! Let not a traitor live!

Antony

Stay, countrymen.

First Plebeian

205 Peace there, hear the noble Antony.

Second Plebeian

We'll hear him, we'll follow him, we'll die with him.

Antony

Good friends, sweet friends, let me not stir you up

To such a sudden flood of mutiny.

They that have done this deed are honourable.

210 What private griefs they have, alas, I know not,

That made them do it. They are wise and honourable,

And will no doubt with reasons answer you.

I come not, friends, to steal away your hearts.

I am no orator, as Brutus is,

215 But—as you know me well—a plain blunt man

That love my friend, and that they know full well

That gave me public leave to speak of him.

For I have neither wit, nor words, nor worth,

Action, nor utterance, nor the power of speech

220 To stir men's blood. I only speak right on.

I tell you that which you yourselves do know,

Show you sweet Caesar's wounds, poor, poor, dumb
   mouths,

And bid them speak for me. But were I Brutus,

And Brutus Antony, there were an Antony

202 *About*: get on with it, bestir yourselves.

208 *flood of mutiny*: wave of violence.

210 *private griefs*: personal grievances.

217 *public . . . speak*: permission to speak in public.
218–20 *I have . . . blood*: Antony claims to be deficient in all branches of (Elizabethan) rhetoric.
218 *wit*: invention, intellectual cleverness.
   words: fluency.
   worth: authority.
220 *right on*: directly.

225 *ruffle up*: stir up, enrage.

225 Would ruffle up your spirits and put a tongue
In every wound of Caesar, that should move
The stones of Rome to rise and mutiny.
    All
We'll mutiny.
    First Plebeian
        We'll burn the house of Brutus.
    Third Plebeian
Away then, come, seek the conspirators.
    Antony
230 Yet hear me, countrymen, yet hear me speak.
    All
Peace ho, hear Antony, most noble Antony!
    Antony
Why, friends, you go to do you know not what.

233 *Wherein*: in what way.

Wherein hath Caesar thus deserv'd your loves?
Alas, you know not! I must tell you then:
235 You have forgot the will I told you of.
    All
Most true. The will, let's stay and hear the will!
    Antony
Here is the will, and under Caesar's seal:
To every Roman citizen he gives,

239 *several*: individual.
drachmaes: silver coins.

To every several man, seventy-five drachmaes.
    Second Plebeian
240 Most noble Caesar, we'll revenge his death!
    Third Plebeian

241 *royal*: generous.

O royal Caesar!
    Antony
Hear me with patience.
    All
Peace ho!
    Antony
Moreover, he hath left you all his walks,

244 *walks*: gardens.
245 *His private arbours*: his own summer-
houses.
new-planted: freshly planted.
247 *common pleasures*: public pleasure-
gardens.
248 *abroad*: in the open air.

245 His private arbours and new-planted orchards,
On this side Tiber; he hath left them you,
And to your heirs for ever—common pleasures,
To walk abroad and recreate yourselves.
Here was a Caesar! When comes such another?
    First Plebeian
250 Never, never! Come, away, away!

251 *the holy place*: the Forum, centre of religious as well as political life in Rome; see 'Shakespeare's Plutarch', p.107.
252 *brands*: burning wood from the funeral pyre.

255 *Pluck*: pull.

257 *afoot*: begun.

263 *upon a wish*: just as I wished. *Fortune*: the goddess Fortune.

266 *Are rid*: have ridden.

267 *Belike*: probably.
267-8 *some . . . them*: some warning about how I have influenced the citizens.

We'll burn his body in the holy place
And with the brands fire the traitors' houses.
Take up the body.
    Second Plebeian
Go fetch fire!
    Third Plebeian
255 Pluck down benches!
    Fourth Plebeian
Pluck down forms, windows, anything!
              [*Exeunt* Plebeians *with the body*
    Antony
Now let it work. Mischief, thou art afoot,
Take thou what course thou wilt!

    Enter Servant

                  How now, fellow?
    Servant
Sir, Octavius is already come to Rome.
    Antony
260 Where is he?
    Servant
He and Lepidus are at Caesar's house.
    Antony
And thither will I straight to visit him.
He comes upon a wish. Fortune is merry,
And in this mood will give us anything.
    Servant
265 I heard him say Brutus and Cassius
Are rid like madmen through the gates of Rome.
    Antony
Belike they had some notice of the people,
How I had mov'd them. Bring me to Octavius.
                    [*Exeunt*

Act 3 Scene 3
Cinna the poet is killed by the angry mob.

1 *tonight*: last night.
2 *things . . . fantasy*: my imagination is filled with ill omens.
3 *will*: desire.
   forth of doors: outside.

12 *you were best*: you had better.

16 *Wisely*: The position of this word allows a double meaning ('with wisdom I say that I am a bachelor'; 'I say that, being wise, I am a bachelor').
18 *bear me a bang*: get a blow from me.

19 *Directly*: The Citizen means 'speaking plainly', but Cinna understands 'immediately'.

SCENE 3

Rome: a street. Enter Cinna the Poet, *and after him the* Plebeians

Cinna the Poet
I dreamt tonight that I did feast with Caesar,
And things unluckily charge my fantasy.
I have no will to wander forth of doors,
Yet something leads me forth.
First Plebeian
5 What is your name?
Second Plebeian
Whither are you going?
Third Plebeian
Where do you dwell?
Fourth Plebeian
Are you a married man or a bachelor?
Second Plebeian
Answer every man directly.
First Plebeian
10 Ay, and briefly.
Fourth Plebeian
Ay, and wisely.
Third Plebeian
Ay, and truly, you were best.
Cinna the Poet
What is my name? Whither am I going? Where do I dwell? Am I a married man or a bachelor? Then to
15 answer every man directly and briefly, wisely and truly. Wisely I say I am a bachelor.
Second Plebeian
That's as much as to say they are fools that marry. You'll bear me a bang for that, I fear. Proceed directly.
Cinna the Poet
Directly I am going to Caesar's funeral.
First Plebeian
20 As a friend or an enemy?
Cinna the Poet
As a friend.

'Tear him to pieces, he's a conspirator.' (3, 3, 27). National Youth Theatre, 1993.

Second Plebeian

That matter is answered directly.

Fourth Plebeian

For your dwelling—briefly.

Cinna the Poet

Briefly, I dwell by the Capitol.

Third Plebeian

25 Your name, sir, truly.

Cinna the Poet

Truly, my name is Cinna.

First Plebeian

Tear him to pieces, he's a conspirator.

Cinna the Poet

I am Cinna the poet, I am Cinna the poet.

Fourth Plebeian

Tear him for his bad verses, tear him for his bad verses.

Cinna the Poet

30 I am not Cinna the conspirator.

Fourth Plebeian

It is no matter, his name's Cinna. Pluck but his name
out of his heart and turn him going.

Third Plebeian

Tear him, tear him! Come, brands ho, firebrands! To
Brutus', to Cassius', burn all! Some to Decius' house, and
35 some to Casca's, some to Ligarius'! Away, go!

Exeunt all the Plebeians *forcing out* Cinna

23 *For your dwelling*: where do you live.

31 *but*: only.
32 *turn him going*: send him on his way.

ACT 4

Act 4 Scene 1
Antony, Octavius, and Lepidus plan their strategy.

SCENE 1

Rome: Antony's *house.* Enter Antony, Octavius, *and* Lepidus

Antony
These many then shall die, their names are **prick'd.**
Octavius
Your brother too must die; consent you, **Lepidus?**
Lepidus
I do consent.
Octavius
            Prick him down, Antony.
Lepidus
Upon condition Publius shall not live,
5 Who is your sister's son, Mark Antony.
Antony
He shall not live—look, with a spot I damn **him.**
But, Lepidus, go you to Caesar's house,
Fetch the will hither, and we shall determine
How to cut off some charge in legacies.
Lepidus
10 What, shall I find you here?
Octavius
Or here or at the Capitol.   [*Exit* **Lepidus**
Antony
This is a slight, unmeritable man,
Meet to be sent on errands; is it fit,
The threefold world divided, he should stand
15 One of the three to share it?
Octavius
               So you thought **him**
And took his voice who should be prick'd **to die**
In our black sentence and proscription.

---

1 *many*: this number.
prick'd: ticked off (with a pin-prick on the list).

4 *Upon condition*: on condition that.

9 *cut . . . legacies*: take some of our expenses out of the legacies in Caesar's will.

11 *Or . . . or*: either . . . or.

12 *slight*: weak.
unmeritable: unworthy.
13 *Meet*: suitable.
fit: right.
14–15 *The . . . share it*: When the world is divided into three parts (Europe, Asia, Africa), he should have one of the shares.
16 *voice*: vote.
prick'd: selected.
17 *In . . . proscription*: in our harsh sentences of death and exile.

18 *I . . . you*: I am older and more experienced than you.

20 *To . . . loads*: to take some of the blame from ourselves.
slanderous: giving cause for slander.
21 *them*: i.e. 'these honours'.

24 *will*: wish.
25 *turn him off*: set him loose.
26 *empty*: unburdened.
shake his ears: i.e. as an ass does when grazing.
27 *commons*: common land belonging to the community.
28 *tried*: experienced.
30 *appoint*: allow.
store of provender: supply of food.
32 *wind*: turn.
33 *His . . . spirit*: the movement of his body being controlled by my mind.
34 *in some taste*: to some extent.
but so: no more than that.
36 *barren-spirited*: with no ideas of his own.
37 *objects*: curiosities.
arts: artefacts.
38 *use*: fashion.
stal'd: worn out.
39 *Begin his fashion*: are the new style for him.
40 *But as a property*: except as an instrument, the means to an end.
42 *levying powers*: raising armies.
straight: immediately.
make head: advance against them.
43 *let . . . combin'd*: let our allied troops be united in one army.
44 *Our . . . stretch'd*: get support from our friends, and make the most of our resources.
45 *presently*: immediately.
sit in counsel: decide in private.
46 *covert . . . disclos'd*: secret problems can be best uncovered.
47 *open . . . answered*: answerèd; obvious dangers safely avoided.
48–9 *at . . . enemies*: tied to a stake and surrounded by baying hounds (like bears in the 'sport' of bear baiting).
51 *mischiefs*: dangerous happenings.

Antony
Octavius, I have seen more days than you,
And though we lay these honours on this man
20 To ease ourselves of divers slanderous loads,
He shall but bear them as the ass bears gold,
To groan and sweat under the business,
Either led or driven, as we point the way;
And having brought our treasure where we will,
25 Then take we down his load and turn him off
(Like to the empty ass) to shake his ears
And graze in commons.
    Octavius
                You may do your will,
But he's a tried and valiant soldier.
    Antony
So is my horse, Octavius, and for that
30 I do appoint him store of provender.
It is a creature that I teach to fight,
To wind, to stop, to run directly on,
His corporal motion govern'd by my spirit.
And, in some taste, is Lepidus but so:
35 He must be taught and train'd and bid go forth,
A barren-spirited fellow, one that feeds
On objects, arts, and imitations,
Which, out of use and stal'd by other men,
Begin his fashion. Do not talk of him
40 But as a property. And now, Octavius,
Listen great things. Brutus and Cassius
Are levying powers; we must straight make head.
Therefore let our alliance be combin'd,
Our best friends made, our means stretch'd,
45 And let us presently go sit in counsel,
How covert matters may be best disclos'd
And open perils surest answered.
    Octavius
Let us do so, for we are at the stake
And bay'd about with many enemies,
50 And some that smile have in their hearts, I fear,
Millions of mischiefs.   *[Exeunt*

Act 4 Scene 2
Brutus and Cassius are beginning to quarrel.

0s.d. *Drum*: The usual accompaniment for troops on the march.

1 *Stand*: halt.

2 *word*: password.

4 *at hand*: near by.
5 *do you salutation*: give you greetings.

7 *In . . . change*: because of some change in himself.
by ill officers: because of the bad conduct of his officers.
8 *worthy*: justifiable.
10 *be satisfied*: be given an explanation.

12 *full of regard*: entirely deserving of respect.

14 *resolv'd*: informed.

16 *familiar instances*: evidence of close friendship.
17 *free . . . conference*: frank and friendly talk.
18 *As . . . old*: that he has shown in the past.

19 *Ever*: always.

Scene 2

Camp near Sardis: outside Brutus's *tent.* **Drum.**
Enter Brutus, Lucilius, Lucius, *and the army.*
Titinius *and* Pindarus *meet them*

Brutus
Stand ho!
Lucilius
Give the word ho, and stand!
Brutus
What now, Lucilius, is Cassius near?
Lucilius
He is at hand, and Pindarus is come
5 To do you salutation from his master.
Brutus
He greets me well. Your master, Pindarus,
In his own change or by ill officers,
Hath given me some worthy cause to wish
Things done undone, but if he be at hand
10 I shall be satisfied.
Pindarus
          I do not doubt
But that my noble master will appear
Such as he is, full of regard and honour.
Brutus
He is not doubted.

Brutus *and* Lucilius *draw apart*

          A word, Lucilius,
How he receiv'd you; let me be resolv'd.
Lucilius
15 With courtesy and with respect enough,
But not with such familiar instances,
Nor with such free and friendly conference,
As he hath used of old.
Brutus
              Thou hast describ'd
A hot friend cooling. Ever note, Lucilius,

21 *enforced*: enforcèd; constrained,
   unnatural.
   ceremony: formality.
22 *tricks*: deceits.
   faith: friendship.
23 *hollow*: insincere.
   hot at hand: eager so long as they are
   held back.
24 *mettle*: spirit.
24s.d. *Low march within*: soft drum-roll
   offstage.
26 *fall*: droop.
   crests: proud necks.
   jades: worthless horses.
27 *Sink in the trial*: fail when they are
   put to the test.
28 *Sardis*: The chief city of Lydia.
29 *horse in general*: main part of the
   cavalry.

20 When love begins to sicken and decay
   It useth an enforced ceremony.
   There are no tricks in plain and simple faith,
   But hollow men, like horses hot at hand,
   Make gallant show and promise of their mettle.

Low march within

25 But when they should endure the bloody spur
   They fall their crests, and like deceitful jades
   Sink in the trial. Comes his army on?
   Lucilius
   They mean this night in Sardis to be quarter'd.
   The greater part, the horse in general,
30 Are come with Cassius.

Enter Cassius *and his powers*

Brutus
                                      Hark, he is arrived.
   March gently on to meet him.
   Cassius
   Stand ho!
   Brutus
   Stand ho, speak the word along!
   First Soldier
   Stand!
   Second Soldier
35 Stand!
   Third Soldier
   Stand!
   Cassius
   Most noble brother, you have done me wrong.
   Brutus
   Judge me, you gods! Wrong I mine enemies?
   And if not so, how should I wrong a brother?
   Cassius
40 Brutus, this sober form of yours hides wrongs,
   And when you do them—

31 *March gently*: advance in a dignified
   manner.

33 *Speak . . . along*: pass the order (to
   halt) along the line.

37 *done me wrong*: injured me.

38 *Wrong I*: do I injure.

40 *sober form*: dignified manner.

41 *content*: calm.

42 *griefs*: grievances.
   softly: quietly.

46 *enlarge your griefs*: tell me your
   grievances freely.
47 *give you audience*: listen to you.

48 *charges*: forces under their command.

50 *do you the like*: you do the same.

Brutus
                    Cassius, be content,
Speak your griefs softly, I do know you well.
Before the eyes of both our armies here—
Which should perceive nothing but love from us—
45 Let us not wrangle. Bid them move away.
Then in my tent, Cassius, enlarge your griefs
And I will give you audience.
    Cassius
                     Pindarus,
Bid our commanders lead their charges off
A little from this ground.
    Brutus
50 Lucius, do you the like, and let no man
Come to our tent till we have done our conference.
Let Lucilius and Titinius guard our door.
                [*Exeunt all but* Brutus *and* Cassius

Act 4 Scene 3
The quarrel continues, although a poet tries
to make peace, until Brutus tells Cassius
that Portia is dead. The armies will march
on to Philippi, but Brutus must first sleep.
Caesar's ghost appears to him.

1 *wrong'd*: injured.
  doth appear: is evident.
2 *condemn'd*: found guilty.
  noted: sentenced.
4 *praying . . . side*: pleading on his
  behalf.
5 *was slighted off*: were dismissed.

8 *nice*: trivial.
  bear . . . comment: get its
  punishment.

10 *condemn'd . . . palm*: criticized for
   taking bribes.
11 *mart*: trade.
   offices: official positions.
12 *undeservers*: men who are not worthy.

SCENE 3

Camp near Sardis: Brutus*'s tent*

Cassius
That you have wrong'd me doth appear in this:
You have condemn'd and noted Lucius Pella
For taking bribes here of the Sardians,
Wherein my letters, praying on his side,
5 Because I knew the man, was slighted off.
    Brutus
You wrong'd yourself to write in such a case.
    Cassius
In such a time as this it is not meet
That every nice offence should bear his comment.
    Brutus
Let me tell you, Cassius, you yourself
10 Are much condemn'd to have an itching palm,
To sell and mart your offices for gold
To undeservers.

'There is no terror, Cassius, in your threats', (*4*, 3, 66). Peter McEnery as Brutus and Emrys James as Cassius, Royal Shakespeare Company, 1983.

Cassius

I, an itching palm?
You know that you are Brutus that speaks this,
Or, by the gods, this speech were else your last.

Brutus

15 The name of Cassius honours this corruption,
And chastisement doth therefore hide his head.

Cassius

Chastisement?

Brutus

Remember March, the Ides of March remember:
Did not great Julius bleed for justice' sake?
20 What villain touch'd his body, that did stab
And not for justice? What, shall one of us,
That struck the foremost man of all this world,
But for supporting robbers, shall we now
Contaminate our fingers with base bribes
25 And sell the mighty space of our large honours
For so much trash as may be grasped thus?
I had rather be a dog and bay the moon
Than such a Roman.

Cassius

Brutus, bait not me,
I'll not endure it. You forget yourself
30 To hedge me in. I am a soldier, I,
Older in practice, abler than yourself
To make conditions.

Brutus

Go to, you are not, Cassius!

Cassius

I am.

Brutus

I say you are not.

Cassius

35 Urge me no more, I shall forget myself.
Have mind upon your health, tempt me no farther!

Brutus

Away, slight man!

Cassius

Is't possible?

---

14 *else*: otherwise.

15–16 *The . . . head*: your name protects this racket, and consequently it doesn't get punished.

20–1 *What . . . justice*: was there a villain who stabbed Caesar for any other reason than the cause of justice.

23 *But . . . robbers*: only because he allowed thieves to go unpunished.

26 *trash*: worthless rubbish.
grasped: graspèd.
thus: Perhaps Brutus shows a clenched fist, grasping at money.
27 *bay*: howl at.
28 *bait*: taunt, provoke; Cassius develops a pun from 'bay'.
29–30 *you . . . in*: you forget who you are, when you try to bind me with your rules.
31 *older in practice*: more experienced in practical matters.
32 *conditions*: agreements, treaties.
Go to: nonsense.

35 *Urge*: test, try.
36 *Have . . . health*: think what's good for you.

39 *give . . . room*: submit.
   rash choler: hasty and fiery temper;
   see 120 note.

42 *Fret*: rage.

44 *budge*: flinch, wince.
45 *observe*: show respectful attention to.

47–8 *You . . . split you*: you can choke
   down your poisonous anger until you
   burst; the spleen was the seat of
   sudden emotions and passions.
48 *forth*: onwards.
49 *mirth*: amusement.

52 *Let . . . so*: let me see it.
53 *mine own part*: myself.

58 *durst*: dare.
   mov'd: angered.

59 *tempted*: tested.

Brutus
                              Hear me, for I will speak.
Must I give way and room to your rash choler?
40 Shall I be frighted when a madman stares?
    Cassius
O ye gods, ye gods, must I endure all this?
    Brutus
All this? Ay, more. Fret till your proud heart break.
Go show your slaves how choleric you are,
And make your bondmen tremble. Must I budge?
45 Must I observe you? Must I stand and crouch
Under your testy humour? By the gods,
You shall digest the venom of your spleen
Though it do split you. For, from this day forth,
I'll use you for my mirth, yea, for my laughter,
50 When you are waspish.
    Cassius
                              Is it come to this?
    Brutus
You say you are a better soldier:
Let it appear so, make your vaunting true
And it shall please me well. For mine own part
I shall be glad to learn of noble men.
    Cassius
55 You wrong me every way, you wrong me, Brutus.
I said an elder soldier, not a better.
Did I say 'better'?
    Brutus
                              If you did, I care not.
    Cassius
When Caesar liv'd, he durst not thus have mov'd **me.**
    Brutus
Peace, peace, you durst not so have tempted him.
    Cassius
60 I durst not?
    Brutus
No.
    Cassius
What? Durst not tempt him?
    Brutus
                              For your life you durst **not.**

63 *presume*: take advantage.

67 *I am . . . honesty*: my integrity
protects me so well.

69 *respect not*: pay no heed to.

71 *vile*: dishonourable.

72–3 *I . . . drachmaes*: I would rather sell
myself and shed my lifeblood for cash:
Brutus's imagery is striking—but the
sense is not easily explained.

73–5 *to wring . . . indirection*: to squeeze
their paltry savings out of the hard-
working (and unwilling) peasants by
some devious trick.

76 *legions*: detachments of troops.

80 *rascal counters*: wretched bits of
metal.

85 *riv'd*: torn.

86 *bear*: accept.
infirmities: weaknesses.

88 *practise*: use.

Cassius
Do not presume too much upon my love,
I may do that I shall be sorry for.
    Brutus
65 You have done that you should be sorry **for.**
There is no terror, Cassius, in your **threats,**
For I am arm'd so strong in honesty
That they pass by me as the idle wind,
Which I respect not. I did send to you
70 For certain sums of gold, which you denied me,
For I can raise no money by vile means.
By heaven, I had rather coin my **heart**
And drop my blood for drachmaes than to **wring**
From the hard hands of peasants their vile **trash**
75 By any indirection. I did send
To you for gold to pay my legions,
Which you denied me. Was that done like Cassius?
Should I have answer'd Caius Cassius so?
When Marcus Brutus grows so covetous
80 To lock such rascal counters from his **friends,**
Be ready, gods, with all your thunderbolts,
Dash him to pieces!
    Cassius
                        I denied you not.
    Brutus
You did.
    Cassius
I did not. He was but a fool that brought
85 My answer back. Brutus hath riv'd my heart.
A friend should bear his friend's infirmities,
But Brutus makes mine greater than they are.
    Brutus
I do not, till you practise them on me.
    Cassius
You love me not.
    Brutus
                  I do not like your faults.
    Cassius
90 A friendly eye could never see such faults.

Brutus
A flatterer's would not, though they do appear
As huge as high Olympus.
  Cassius
Come, Antony, and young Octavius, come,
Revenge yourselves alone on Cassius,
95 For Cassius is a-weary of the world:
Hated by one he loves, brav'd by his brother,
Check'd like a bondman, all his faults observ'd,
Set in a notebook, learn'd, and conn'd by rote,
To cast into my teeth. O, I could weep
100 My spirit from mine eyes! There is my dagger
And here my naked breast: within, a heart
Dearer than Pluto's mine, richer than gold.
If that thou beest a Roman take it forth,
I that denied thee gold will give my heart:
105 Strike as thou didst at Caesar. For I know
When thou didst hate him worst thou loved'st him
        better
Than ever thou lov'd'st Cassius.
  Brutus
                                 Sheathe your dagger.
Be angry when you will, it shall have scope;
Do what you will, dishonour shall be humour.
110 O Cassius, you are yoked with a lamb
That carries anger as the flint bears fire,
Who, much enforced, shows a hasty spark
And straight is cold again.
  Cassius
                          Hath Cassius liv'd
To be but mirth and laughter to his Brutus
115 When grief and blood ill-temper'd vexeth him?
  Brutus
When I spoke that, I was ill-temper'd too.
  Cassius
Do you confess so much? Give me your hand.
  Brutus
And my heart too.
  Cassius
                    O Brutus!

92 *Olympus*: the mountain home of the Greek gods.

94 *alone*: only.

96 *brav'd*: defied.
97 *Check'd*: rebuked.
98 *conn'd by rote*: learned by heart.
99 *To . . . teeth*: to repeat to my face.
99–100 *weep . . . eyes*: die of grief.

102 *Dearer*: more precious.
Pluto's mine: Cassius means *Plutus*, god of riches; but his name was often confused (as here) with that of *Pluto*, the god of the underworld.

108 *scope*: free expression.
109 *dishonour . . . humour*: I shall take your abuse as a mere whim.
110 *yoked*: yokèd; allied with, teamed up with.
111–13 *carries . . . again*: has anger inside him—just as a flint holds fire: striking either of them will give a brief spark that cools down immediately.
112 *enforced*: enforcèd.

115 *ill-temper'd*: badly mixed together; Cassius refers to the mixture of 'grief and blood'—but Brutus uses the expression in the modern sense (= bad-tempered).

117 *confess*: admit.

Brutus

What's the matter?

Cassius

Have not you love enough to bear with me

120 When that rash humour which my mother gave me

Makes me forgetful?

Brutus

Yes, Cassius, and from henceforth

When you are over-earnest with your Brutus,

He'll think your mother chides, and leave you so.

Enter a Poet, Lucilius, *and* Titinius

Poet

Let me go in to see the generals.

125 There is some grudge between 'em, 'tis not meet

They be alone.

Lucilius

You shall not come to them.

Poet

Nothing but death shall stay me.

Cassius

How now, what's the matter?

Poet

130 For shame, you generals, what do you mean?

Love and be friends, as two such men should be,

For I have seen more years, I'm sure, than ye.

Cassius

Ha, ha, how vildly doth this cynic rhyme!

Brutus

Get you hence, sirrah; saucy fellow, hence!

Cassius

135 Bear with him, Brutus, 'tis his fashion.

Brutus

I'll know his humour when he knows his time.

What should the wars do with these jigging fools?

Companion, hence!

Cassius

Away, away, be gone! [*Exit* Poet

---

119 *bear with me*: be patient with me.

120 *rash humour*: i.e. choler, one of the four 'humours' or temperaments (see *5, 5, 73*); Brutus has already referred to Cassius's 'rash choler' (line 39), and to his being 'choleric' (line 43).

121 *forgetful*: forget myself.

123 *chides*: scolds.
leave you so: leave it at that.

125 *grudge*: quarrel.
meet: right.

128 *stay*: stop.

132 *ye*: you.

133 *vildly*: terribly.
cynic: would-be philosopher.

134 *sirrah*: A form of address expressing contempt.

135 *'tis his fashion*: it's just his way.

136 *I'll . . . time*: I will allow him his eccentricity ('humour') when he recognizes that there is a proper occasion for it.

137 *jigging fools*: idiot rhymesters; see 'Shakespeare's Plutarch', p.108.

138 *Companion*: fellow.

140 *lodge*: pitch camp for.

144 *sick . . . griefs*: weary because of many problems.

145 *Of . . . use*: you're not being true to your philosophical beliefs; Brutus explains something of the Stoic philosophy of patient endurance in 5, 1, 103–7.
146 *give place*: surrender.
   accidental: happening by chance.
147–56 *Portia . . . fire*: What appears to be Shakespeare's first draft of these lines remains below (181–95).

150 *scap'd I killing*: did I avoid being killed.
   cross'd: angered.
151 *O insupportable . . . loss*: What an unbearable loss of someone so very close ('touching') to you.
152 *Upon*: of.
   Impatient of: unable or unwilling to endure.
154 *with her death*: with the news of her death.
155 *fell distract*: went out of her mind.
156 *swallow'd fire*: Plutarch says that Portia 'took hot burning coals and cast them into her mouth'.

Brutus
Lucilius and Titinius, bid the commanders
140 Prepare to lodge their companies tonight.
   Cassius
And come yourselves, and bring Messala with you
Immediately to us.   [*Exeunt* Lucilius *and* Titinius
   Brutus
[*To* Lucius *within*] Lucius, a bowl of wine!
   Cassius
I did not think you could have been so angry.
   Brutus
O Cassius, I am sick of many griefs.
   Cassius
145 Of your philosophy you make no use
If you give place to accidental evils.
   Brutus
No man bears sorrow better. Portia is dead.
   Cassius
Ha? Portia?
   Brutus
She is dead.
   Cassius
150 How scap'd I killing when I cross'd you so?
O insupportable and touching loss!
Upon what sickness?
   Brutus
                    Impatient of my absence,
And grief that young Octavius with Mark Antony
Have made themselves so strong—for with her death
155 That tidings came. With this she fell distract
And, her attendants absent, swallow'd fire.
   Cassius
And died so?
   Brutus
                    Even so.
   Cassius
                              O ye immortal gods!

157s.d. *tapers*: candles.

157 *unkindness*: bad (unnatural) feelings.

161 *o'erswell*: overflow.

165 *call . . . necessities*: ask ourselves what needs to be done.

167 *received*: receivèd.

169 *Come . . . us*: are advancing upon us.

170 *Bending their expedition*: heading quickly.

172 *what addition*: anything else.

173 *proscription*: The *proscriptio* was a list of Roman citizens who were declared outlaws and whose goods were confiscated.
bills: orders.

Enter Boy Lucius *with wine and tapers*

Brutus
Speak no more of her. Give me a bowl of wine.
In this I bury all unkindness, Cassius. [*Drinks*]
Cassius
160 My heart is thirsty for that noble pledge.
Fill, Lucius, till the wine o'erswell the cup,
I cannot drink too much of Brutus' love. [*Drinks*]
[*Exit* Lucius

Enter Titinius *and* Messala

Brutus
Come in, Titinius; welcome, good Messala.
Now sit we close about this taper here
165 And call in question our necessities.
Cassius
Portia, art thou gone?
Brutus
No more, I pray you.
Messala, I have here received letters
That young Octavius and Mark Antony
Come down upon us with a mighty power,
170 Bending their expedition toward Philippi.
Messala
Myself have letters of the selfsame tenor.
Brutus
With what addition?
Messala
That by proscription and bills of outlawry
Octavius, Antony, and Lepidus
175 Have put to death an hundred senators.
Brutus
Therein our letters do not well agree:
Mine speak of seventy senators that died
By their proscriptions, Cicero being one.
Cassius
Cicero one?

Messala

Cicero is dead,

180 And by that order of proscription.

Had you your letters from your wife, my lord?

Brutus

No, Messala.

Messala

Nor nothing in your letters writ of her?

Brutus

Nothing, Messala.

Messala

That, methinks, is strange.

Brutus

185 Why ask you? Hear you aught of her in yours?

Messala

No, my lord.

Brutus

Now as you are a Roman tell me true.

Messala

Then like a Roman bear the truth I tell,

For certain she is dead, and by strange manner.

Brutus

190 Why, farewell, Portia. We must die, Messala.

With meditating that she must die once,

I have the patience to endure it now.

Messala

Even so, great men great losses should endure.

Cassius

I have as much of this in art as you,

195 But yet my nature could not bear it so.

Brutus

Well, to our work alive. What do you think

Of marching to Philippi presently?

Cassius

I do not think it good.

Brutus

Your reason?

Cassius

This it is:

'Tis better that the enemy seek us,

200 So shall he waste his means, weary his soldiers,

181–95 *Had you . . . so*: Perhaps Shakespeare thought he had made Brutus too stoical in this acceptance of Portia's death, and (forgetting to cancel his first version) added the lines that now appear as 147–9.

183 *writ of*: written about.

185 *aught*: anything.

191 *once*: in any case.

193 *Even so*: just like this.

194 *I have . . . you*: I know as much as you do about the need for patient endurance.

196 *alive*: with our living energy.

197 *presently*: immediately.

200 *waste*: exhaust.
     means: supplies.

201 *Doing himself offence*: harming
himself.
lying still: staying in the same place.

203 *of force*: necessarily.

205 *forc'd*: enforced, compelled.

206 *grudg'd us contribution*: been
unwilling to give us supplies.
207 *by them*: through their land.
208 *By them*: from them.
make . . . up: increase the size of his
army.
209 *Come on*: advance.
new-added: reinforced.

214 *tried . . . friends*: we have asked our
allies for all the help they can give.
215 *Our . . . brimful*: our armies are as
large as they need to be.
our . . . ripe: this is the right moment
to fight for our cause.
217 *at the height*: i.e. of strength and
fortune.
219 *flood*: high tide.
220 *Omitted*: if men fail to take the
opportunity presented to them.
221 *bound in shallows*: stranded in
shallow water.
223 *serves*: is best for us.
224 *ventures*: enterprises (goods risked in
trade).
with: at.

226 *The deep . . . talk*: it's got late into
the night whilst we've been talking.
227–8 *nature . . . rest*: human nature must
give way to its needs, and we will at
least satisfy these with a little rest.
228 *niggard*: be sparing with.

Doing himself offence, whilst we, lying still,
Are full of rest, defence, and nimbleness.
   Brutus
Good reasons must of force give place to better:
The people 'twixt Philippi and this ground
205 Do stand but in a forc'd affection,
For they have grudg'd us contribution.
The enemy, marching along by them,
By them shall make a fuller number up,
Come on refresh'd, new added, and encourag'd,
210 From which advantage shall we cut him off
If at Philippi we do face him there,
These people at our back.
   Cassius
                      Hear me, good brother.
   Brutus
Under your pardon. You must note beside
That we have tried the utmost of our friends,
215 Our legions are brimful, our cause is ripe;
The enemy increaseth every day,
We, at the height, are ready to decline.
There is a tide in the affairs of men
Which, taken at the flood, leads on to fortune;
220 Omitted, all the voyage of their life
Is bound in shallows and in miseries.
On such a full sea are we now afloat,
And we must take the current when it serves
Or lose our ventures.
   Cassius
                  Then with your will go on,
225 We'll along ourselves and meet them at Philippi.
   Brutus
The deep of night is crept upon our talk,
And nature must obey necessity,
Which we will niggard with a little rest.
There is no more to say?
   Cassius
               No more. Good night.
230 Early tomorrow will we rise and hence.
   Brutus
Lucius!

Enter Lucius

231 *gown*: dressing-gown.

       My gown.   [*Exit* Lucius
      Farewell, good Messala.
Good night, Titinius. Noble, noble Cassius,
Good night and good repose.
    Cassius
               O my dear brother!
This was an ill beginning of the night.
235 Never come such division 'tween our souls!
Let it not, Brutus.

Enter Lucius *with the gown*

Brutus
           Everything is well.
    Cassius
Good night, my lord.
    Brutus
            Good night, good brother.
Titinius and **Messala**
Good night, Lord Brutus.
    Brutus
           Farewell every one.
        [*Exeunt* Cassius, Titinius, **Messala**
Give me the gown. Where is thy instrument?
    Lucius
240 Here in the tent.
    Brutus
          What, thou speak'st drowsily.

241 *knave*: lad (Brutus is affectionate).
o'erwatched: wearied through being
kept awake too long.

Poor knave, I blame thee not, thou art o'erwatch'd.
Call Claudio and some other of my men,
I'll have them sleep on cushions in my tent.
    Lucius
Varrus and Claudio!

Enter Varrus *and* Claudio

Varrus

245 Calls my lord?

Brutus

I pray you, sirs, lie in my tent and sleep,
It may be I shall raise you by and by
On business to my brother Cassius.

Varrus

So please you, we will stand and watch your pleasure.

Brutus

250 I will not have it so. Lie down, good sirs,
It may be I shall otherwise bethink me.

Varrus *and* Claudio *lie down*

Look, Lucius, here's the book I sought for so,
I put it in the pocket of my gown.

Lucius

I was sure your lordship did not give it me.

Brutus

255 Bear with me, good boy, I am much forgetful.
Canst thou hold up thy heavy eyes awhile
And touch thy instrument a strain or two?

Lucius

Ay, my lord, an't please you.

Brutus

                                    It does, my boy.
I trouble thee too much, but thou art willing.

Lucius

260 It is my duty, sir.

Brutus

I should not urge thy duty past thy might,
I know young bloods look for a time of rest.

Lucius

I have slept, my lord, already.

Brutus

It was well done and thou shalt sleep again,
265 I will not hold thee long. If I do live
I will be good to thee.

247 *raise*: rouse.
248 *On business*: to go on business.

249 *watch your pleasure*: stay awake until you need us.

251 *otherwise bethink me*: decide to do something else.

257 *touch . . . two*: play one or two tunes on your instrument (probably a lute).

258 *an't*: if it.
262 *bloods*: constitutions.
    look for: need.

265 *hold*: keep.

Music, and a song

This is a sleepy tune. O murd'rous slumber,
Layest thou thy leaden mace upon my boy,
That plays thee music? Gentle knave, good night,
270   I will not do thee so much wrong to wake thee.
If thou dost nod thou break'st thy instrument.
I'll take it from thee and, good boy, good night.
Let me see, let me see, is not the leaf turn'd down
Where I left reading? Here it is, I think.

Enter the Ghost of Caesar

275   How ill this taper burns! Ha, who comes here?
I think it is the weakness of mine eyes
That shapes this monstrous apparition.
It comes upon me. Art thou any thing?
Art thou some god, some angel, or some devil,
280   That mak'st my blood cold and my hair to stare?
Speak to me what thou art.
    Ghost
Thy evil spirit, Brutus.
    Brutus
                                Why com'st thou?
    Ghost
To tell thee thou shalt see me at Philippi.
    Brutus
Well, then I shall see thee again?
    Ghost
285   Ay, at Philippi.
    Brutus
Why, I will see thee at Philippi then.   [*Exit* Ghost
Now I have taken heart thou vanishest.
Ill spirit, I would hold more talk with thee.
Boy, Lucius! Varrus! Claudio! Sirs, awake!
290   Claudio!
    Lucius
The strings, my lord, are false.
    Brutus
He thinks he still is at his instrument.
Lucius, awake!

268-9 *Layest . . . music*: Brutus images sleep as an officer of the law who arrests Lucius by touching him on the shoulder with a heavy mace (the usual Elizabethan form of arrest).

278 *upon*: towards.
     any thing: a thing of substance, real.
280 *stare*: stand on end.

287 *taken heart*: recovered my courage.
288 *would hold*: would like to have.

291 *false*: out of tune.

Lucius
My lord?

Brutus
295 Didst thou dream, Lucius, that thou so cried'st out?

Lucius
My lord, I do not know that I did cry.

Brutus
Yes, that thou didst. Didst thou see anything?

Lucius
Nothing, my lord.

Brutus
Sleep again, Lucius. Sirrah Claudio!
300 [*To* Varrus] Fellow, thou, awake!

Varrus
My lord?

Claudio
My lord?

Brutus
Why did you so cry out, sirs, in your sleep?

Both
Did we, my lord?

Brutus
                    Ay. Saw you anything?

Varrus
305 No, my lord, I saw nothing.

Claudio
                              Nor I, my lord.

Brutus
Go and commend me to my brother Cassius.
Bid him set on his powers betimes before,
And we will follow.

Both
                              It shall be done, my lord.   [*Exeunt*

306 *commend me*: present my compliments to.
307 *set on his powers*: order his troops to advance.
betimes: early.
before: i.e. before my soldiers.

'A peevish schoolboy . . . Join'd with a masker and a reveller.', (5, 1, 61–2). Nigel Cooke as Octavius, Peter McEnery as Brutus, Emrys James as Cassius, and David Schofield as Antony, Royal Shakespeare Company, 1983.

Act 5 Scene 1
Brief confrontation, then both sides prepare
for battle. Cassius has seen omens; he will
die rather than surrender, and says farewell
to Brutus.

1 *answered*: answerèd; fulfilled
(Octavius is being ironic; the opposite
of what they hoped for has happened).
3 *keep*: remain in.
4 *battles*: troops in battle formation.
5 *warn*: resist.
6 *Answering . . . them*: responding to
our challenge before it is made.

7 *Tut, I am . . . bosoms*: don't worry; I
know what is in their minds.
8–9 *They . . . places*: they would prefer
to approach from different directions.
9 *come down*: make a surprise attack.
10 *fearful*: frightened; frightening. The
word is capable of both, or either, of
these senses.
bravery: defiance.
face: appearance.

14 *bloody . . . battle*: Plutarch refers to
the 'signal of battle' as 'an arming
scarlet coat'—i.e. a vest of rich
material embroidered with heraldic
devices, worn over the armour.
15 *something . . . done*: some action will
have to be taken.

19 *cross*: oppose.
exigent: critical occasion.

SCENE 1

The plains of Philippi: enter Octavius, Antony, *and
their army*

Octavius
Now, Antony, our hopes are answered.
You said the enemy would not come down
But keep the hills and upper regions.
It proves not so: their battles are at hand,
5 They mean to warn us at Philippi here,
Answering before we do demand of them.
    Antony
Tut, I am in their bosoms, and I know
Wherefore they do it. They could be content
To visit other places and come down
10 With fearful bravery, thinking by this face
To fasten in our thoughts that they have courage.
But 'tis not so.

Enter a Messenger

Messenger
           Prepare you, generals,
The enemy comes on in gallant show,
Their bloody sign of battle is hung out,
15 And something to be done immediately.
    Antony
Octavius, lead your battle softly on
Upon the left hand of the even field.
    Octavius
Upon the right hand I, keep thou the left.
    Antony
Why do you cross me in this exigent?
    Octavius
20 I do not cross you, but I will do so.

March

Drum. Enter Brutus, Cassius, *and their army;*
Lucilius, Titinius, Messala, *and others*

Brutus
They stand and would have parley.
Cassius
Stand fast, Titinius, we must out and talk.
Octavius
Mark Antony, shall we give sign of battle?
Antony
No, Caesar, we will answer on their charge.
25 Make forth, the generals would have some words.
Octavius
Stir not until the signal.
Brutus
Words before blows; is it so, countrymen?
Octavius
Not that we love words better, as you do.
Brutus
Good words are better than bad strokes, Octavius.
Antony
30 In your bad strokes, Brutus, you give good words.
Witness the hole you made in Caesar's heart,
Crying, 'Long live, hail, Caesar!'
Cassius
                                        Antony,
The posture of your blows are yet unknown;
But for your words, they rob the Hybla bees
35 And leave them honeyless.
Antony
                                Not stingless too?
Brutus
O yes, and soundless too,
For you have stolen their buzzing, Antony,
And very wisely threat before you sting.
Antony
Villains! You did not so when your vile daggers
40 Hack'd one another in the sides of Caesar.
You show'd your teeth like apes and fawn'd like hounds,

---

21 *parley*: conference.

22 *Stand fast*: halt.

24 *charge*: attack.
25 *Make forth*: go forward.

31 *Witness*: as can be seen from.

33 *posture . . . unknown*: we don't know
what kind of blows you strike;
'posture' = the position of a weapon in
warfare.
34 *Hybla*: A town in Sicily famous for
honey.

38 *threat*: threaten.

39 *so*: i.e. threaten before they stabbed
Caesar.
41 *show'd your teeth*: grinned.

43 *damned*: damnèd.

45 *thank yourself*: you have only yourself
to thank (for this insult).

47 *rul'd*: had his way.

48 *cause*: come to the point.

49 *proof*: deciding the argument in
battle.
redder drops: drops of blood.

52 *goes up*: is sheathed.

54 *another Caesar*: i.e. himself.

55 *Have . . . traitors*: has increased the
slaughter done by traitors.

57 *Unless . . . thee*: unless they are in
your army; Brutus insists that the
rebels are still loyal to Rome.

59 *strain*: family.
60 *honourable*: i.e. honourably.

61 *peevish*: silly, foolish.
schoolboy: Octavius was only eighteen
when Julius Caesar was assassinated.
worthless: unworthy.
62 *masker*: one who takes part in masked
entertainments.

66 *stomachs*: appetites for fighting.

67 *swim bark*: let the ship sail (i.e.
whatever happens we must fight).
68 *on the hazard*: at risk.

And bow'd like bondmen, kissing Caesar's feet,
Whilst damned Casca, like a cur, behind
Struck Caesar on the neck. O you flatterers!
Cassius
45 Flatterers? Now, Brutus, thank yourself.
This tongue had not offended so today
If Cassius might have rul'd.
Octavius
Come, come, the cause. If arguing make us sweat,
The proof of it will turn to redder drops.
50 Look,
I draw a sword against conspirators;
When think you that the sword goes up again?
Never, till Caesar's three and thirty wounds
Be well aveng'd, or till another Caesar
55 Have added slaughter to the sword of traitors.
Brutus
Caesar, thou canst not die by traitors' hands
Unless thou bring'st them with thee.
Octavius
        So I hope.
I was not born to die on Brutus' sword.
Brutus
O, if thou wert the noblest of thy strain,
60 Young man, thou couldst not die more honourable.
Cassius
A peevish schoolboy, worthless of such honour,
Join'd with a masker and a reveller!
Antony
Old Cassius still!
Octavius
      Come, Antony, away!
Defiance, traitors, hurl we in your teeth.
65 If you dare fight today, come to the field;
If not, when you have stomachs.
       [*Exeunt* Octavius, Antony, *and army*
Cassius
Why now blow wind, swell billow, and swim bark!
The storm is up, and all is on the hazard.
Brutus
Ho, Lucilius, hark, a word with you.

Lucilius *and* Messala *stand forth*

Lucilius
My lord.

Brutus *speaks apart to* Lucilius

Cassius
70 Messala!
Messala
What says my general?
Cassius
Messala,
This is my birthday, as this very day
Was Cassius born. Give me thy hand, Messala.
Be thou my witness that against my will
(As Pompey was) am I compell'd to set
75 Upon one battle all our liberties.
You know that I held Epicurus strong
And his opinion. Now I change my mind
And partly credit things that do presage.
Coming from Sardis, on our former ensign
80 Two mighty eagles fell, and there they perch'd,
Gorging and feeding from our soldiers' hands,
Who to Philippi here consorted us.
This morning are they fled away and gone,
And in their steads do ravens, crows, and kites
85 Fly o'er our heads and downward look on us
As we were sickly prey. Their shadows seem
A canopy most fatal under which
Our army lies, ready to give up the ghost.
Messala
Believe not so.
Cassius
I but believe it partly,
90 For I am fresh of spirit and resolv'd
To meet all perils very constantly.
Brutus
Even so, Lucilius. [*Advancing*]

74 *Pompey*: At the battle of Pharsalia
Pompey was compelled to fight
against his better judgement; he was
defeated.
set: risk.
76–7 *I held . . . opinion*: I once believed
firmly in the teaching of Epicurus (a
Greek philosopher who thought that
belief in omens was mere
superstition); see 'Shakespeare's
Plutarch', p.109.
78 *credit . . . presage*: believe in things
that foretell the future.
79 *former*: foremost.
ensign: standard.

80 *fell*: alighted.
82 *consorted*: accompanied.
84 *steads*: places.
86 *As . . . prey*: as though we would soon
be prey for them.
87 *fatal*: foreboding, signifying death
(like the canopy over a bier).
88 *give . . . ghost*: die.
89 *but . . . partly*: only half believe it.
90 *fresh of spirit*: hopeful in my mind.
91 *constantly*: with courage.
92 *Even so*: Brutus gives an instruction to
Lucilius before coming to the front of
the stage.

93 *The . . . friendly*: may the gods be on
our side.
94 *Lovers*: good friends.
lead . . . age: live to old age.
95 *rests*: remain.
still: always.
96 *reason . . . befall*: decide what to do if
the worst happens.
99 *determined*: determinèd.

100–2 *Even . . . himself*: I shall act in
accordance with the same philosophy
that made me censure Cato (Portia's
father) for killing himself (see
2, 1, 295). Brutus himself explains
the main tenet of Stoicism in lines
103–7.
104–5 *For . . . life*: to forestall ('prevent')
the natural course of life because one
is afraid of what might befall ('fall').
105 *arming*: fortifying.
106 *stay*: wait.
high powers: the gods.

108–9 *led . . . Rome*: Roman commanders
celebrated their achievements by
leading their prisoners in procession
through the streets of Rome.

111 *bound*: in bondage.

115 *everlasting*: eternal, final.

Cassius
                              Now, most noble Brutus,
The gods today stand friendly that we may,
Lovers in peace, lead on our days to age!
95 But since the affairs of men rests still incertain,
Let's reason with the worst that may befall.
If we do lose this battle, then is this
The very last time we shall speak together.
What are you then determined to do?
        Brutus
100 Even by the rule of that philosophy
By which I did blame Cato for the death
Which he did give himself—I know not how,
But I do find it cowardly and vile,
For fear of what might fall, so to prevent
105 The time of life—arming myself with patience
To stay the providence of some high powers
That govern us below.
        Cassius
                              Then if we lose this battle,
You are contented to be led in triumph
Through the streets of Rome?
        Brutus
110 No, Cassius, no. Think not, thou noble Roman,
That ever Brutus will go bound to Rome:
He bears too great a mind. But this same day
Must end that work the Ides of March begun.
And whether we shall meet again I know not,
115 Therefore our everlasting farewell take:
For ever and for ever, farewell, Cassius!
If we do meet again, why, we shall smile;
If not, why then this parting was well made.
        Cassius
For ever and for ever, farewell, Brutus!
120 If we do meet again, we'll smile indeed;
If not, 'tis true this parting was well made.
        Brutus
Why then, lead on. O, that a man might know
The end of this day's business ere it come!
But it sufficeth that the day will end,
And then the end is known. Come ho, away!   [*Exeunt*

Act 5 Scene 2
Battle has commenced—and Brutus is
hopeful.

Os.d. *Alarum*: trumpet signal for attack.

1 *bills*: written orders.
2 *other side*: i.e. the troops led by
Cassius.

3 *set on*: charge.
4 *cold demeanour*: faint courage.
  wing: troops.
5 *push*: attack.
  overthrow: defeat.

Act 5 Scene 3
Cassius orders his slave to kill him, and
Titinius finds his body. Brutus fights on.

1 *the villains*: i.e. his own men.
2 *Myself . . . enemy*: I have become the
enemy to my own men.
3 *ensign*: standard bearer.
4 *it*: i.e. the standard.

6 *on*: over.
7 *fell to spoil*: started to plunder.
8 *all enclos'd*: quite surrounded.

10 *tents*: camp.

SCENE 2

The field of battle. Alarum. Enter Brutus *and*
Messala

Brutus
Ride, ride, Messala, ride, and give these bills
Unto the legions on the other side.

Loud alarum

Let them set on at once, for I perceive
But cold demeanour in Octavio's wing,
5 And sudden push gives them the overthrow.
Ride, ride, Messala, let them all come down.   [*Exeunt*

SCENE 3

Another part of the field. Alarums. Enter Cassius *and*
Titinius

Cassius
O, look, Titinius, look, the villains fly!
Myself have to mine own turn'd enemy.
This ensign here of mine was turning back;
I slew the coward and did take it from him.
Titinius
5 O Cassius, Brutus gave the word too early,
Who, having some advantage on Octavius,
Took it too eagerly. His soldiers fell to spoil
Whilst we by Antony are all enclos'd.

Enter Pindarus

Pindarus
Fly further off, my lord, fly further off!
10 Mark Antony is in your tents, my lord,
Fly therefore, noble Cassius, fly far off.

Cassius
This hill is far enough. Look, look, Titinius,
Are those my tents where I perceive the fire?
    Titinius
They are, my lord.
    Cassius
                    Titinius, if thou lovest me,
15 Mount thou my horse and hide thy spurs in him
Till he have brought thee up to yonder troops
And here again that I may rest assur'd
Whether yond troops are friend or enemy.
    Titinius
I will be here again even with a thought.   *[Exit*
    Cassius
20 Go, Pindarus, get higher on that hill,
My sight was ever thick: regard Titinius
And tell me what thou not'st about the field.

    Pindarus *goes up*

This day I breathed first, time is come round
And where I did begin there shall I end:
25 My life is run his compass. Sirrah, what news?
    Pindarus
[*Above*] O my lord!
    Cassius
What news?
    Pindarus
Titinius is enclosed round about
With horsemen that make to him on the spur,
30 Yet he spurs on. Now they are almost on him.
Now Titinius—Now some light; O, he lights too.
He's ta'en. [*Shout*] And hark, they shout for joy.
    Cassius
Come down, behold no more.
O, coward that I am to live so long
35 To see my best friend ta'en before my face.

    Pindarus *descends*

---

12 *far*: further.

15 *hide thy spurs*: dig your spurs in deeply.

17 *rest assur'd*: know.

18 *yond*: yonder.

19 *even . . . thought*: as quick as a thought.

21 *My . . . thick*: I have always been short-sighted.
regard: watch.
22 *not'st*: see.

23 *breathed*: breathèd.

25 *is run his compass*: has come full circle.

28 *enclosed*: enclosèd; surrounded.
29 *on the spur*: spurring their horses.

31 *light*: alight, dismount.

37   *In Parthia . . . prisoner*: Cassius had
been fighting under the command of
Crassus in 53 BC (see 'About the Play,
p.v).
38   *I swore . . . life*: I made you swear, in
return for saving your life.
41   *be a freeman*: set yourself free from
slavery.
42   *search*: probe down into.
43   *hilts*: handle of the sword.

48   *Durst . . . will*: if I had dared to do
what I wanted.

50   *note*: notice.

51   *but change*: only exchange.

54   *tidings*: news.

Come hither, sirrah.
In Parthia did I take thee prisoner,
And then I swore thee, saving of thy life,
That whatsoever I did bid thee do
40   Thou shouldst attempt it. Come now, keep thine oath.
Now be a freeman, and with this good sword,
That ran through Caesar's bowels, search this bosom.
Stand not to answer; here, take thou the hilts
And when my face is cover'd, as 'tis now,
45   Guide thou the sword.

      Pindarus *stabs him*

                    Caesar, thou art reveng'd
Even with the sword that kill'd thee.   [*Dies*
    Pindarus
So I am free, yet would not so have been
Durst I have done my will. O Cassius,
Far from this country Pindarus shall run,
50   Where never Roman shall take note of him.   [*Exit*

      Enter Titinius *and* Messala

    Messala
It is but change, Titinius, for Octavius
Is overthrown by noble Brutus' power,
As Cassius' legions are by Antony.
    Titinius
These tidings will well comfort Cassius.
    Messala
55   Where did you leave him?
    Titinius
                    All disconsolate
With Pindarus his bondman, on this hill.
    Messala
Is not that he that lies upon the ground?
    Titinius
He lies not like the living. O my heart!
    Messala
Is not that he?

Titinius

  No, this was he, Messala,
60 But Cassius is no more. O setting sun,
  As in thy red rays thou dost sink to night,
  So in his red blood Cassius' day is set.
  The sun of Rome is set. Our day is gone,
  Clouds, dews, and dangers come. Our deeds are done.
65 Mistrust of my success hath done this deed.

Messala

  Mistrust of good success hath done this deed.
  O hateful error, melancholy's child,
  Why dost thou show to the apt thoughts of men
  The things that are not? O error, soon conceiv'd,
70 Thou never com'st unto a happy birth
  But kill'st the mother that engender'd thee.

Titinius

  What, Pindarus? Where art thou, Pindarus?

Messala

  Seek him, Titinius, whilst I go to meet
  The noble Brutus, thrusting this report
75 Into his ears. I may say 'thrusting' it,
  For piercing steel and darts envenomed
  Shall be as welcome to the ears of Brutus
  As tidings of this sight.

Titinius

                Hie you, Messala,
  And I will seek for Pindarus the while.   [*Exit* Messala
80 Why didst thou send me forth, brave Cassius?
  Did I not meet thy friends? And did not they
  Put on my brows this wreath of victory
  And bid me give it thee? Didst thou not hear their
    shouts?
  Alas, thou hast misconstrued everything.
85 But hold thee, take this garland on thy brow;
  Thy Brutus bid me give it thee, and I
  Will do his bidding. Brutus, come apace,
  And see how I regarded Caius Cassius.
  By your leave, gods!—This is a Roman's part.
90 Come, Cassius' sword, and find Titinius' heart.   [*Dies*

64 *dews*: the dew of evening.
65 *Mistrust*: doubt.

67–71 *O hateful error . . . thee*: Messala's exaggerated rhetoric shows his outrage at the *unnecessary* death of Cassius.
67 *melancholy's child*: the offspring of depression.
68 *apt*: ready (to believe the worst).
69 *soon conceiv'd*: quickly imagined.
70-1 *Thou . . . thee*: nothing good ever comes from a mistake; it's more likely to ruin the person who makes it.
71 *engender'd*: gave birth to.

76 *darts envenomed*: envenomèd; poisoned arrows.

78 *Hie*: hasten.

80 *brave*: noble.

82 *wreath of victory*: wreath of oak leaves given a victorious warrior.

84 *misconstrued*: misinterpreted.
85 *hold thee*: wait.

88 *how*: how highly.
89 *By . . . gods*: Titinius asks pardon from the gods for ending his life prematurely.
a Roman's part: what is expected of a Roman.

Alarum. Enter Brutus, Messala, Young Cato, Strato,
Volumnius, *and* Lucilius, Labeo, *and* Flavius

Brutus
Where, where, Messala, doth his body lie?
    Messala
Lo yonder, and Titinius mourning it.
    Brutus
Titinius' face is upward.
    Cato
                            He is slain.
    Brutus
O Julius Caesar, thou art mighty yet,
95 Thy spirit walks abroad and turns our swords
In our own proper entrails.

Low alarums

Cato
                            Brave Titinius!
Look whe'er he have not crown'd dead Cassius.
    Brutus
Are yet two Romans living such as these?
The last of all the Romans, fare thee well!
100 It is impossible that ever Rome
Should breed thy fellow. Friends, I owe mo tears
To this dead man than you shall see me pay.
I shall find time, Cassius, I shall find time.
Come therefore and to Thasos send his body;
105 His funerals shall not be in our camp
Lest it discomfort us. Lucilius, come,
And come, young Cato, let us to the field.
Labeo and Flavio, set our battles on.
'Tis three o'clock, and, Romans, yet ere night
110 We shall try fortune in a second fight.   [*Exeunt*

95 *abroad*: at large.
96 *own proper*: very own.

96s.d. *Low alarums*: subdued trumpet-
    calls, signalling defeat or surrender.

97 *whe'er*: whether, if he hasn't (the tone
    is admiring).
98 *yet*: still.
99 *The . . . Romans*: the last man worthy
    to be called a Roman.
101 *thy fellow*: your equal, a man like you.
    mo: more.

104 *Thasos*: An island in the Aegean Sea,
    not far from Philippi.
105 *funerals*: funeral ceremonies.
106 *discomfort*: dishearten.
107 *field*: battlefield.
108 *set . . . on*: set our troops in battle
    array.
109 *ere*: before.
110 *try fortune*: try our luck.

SCENE 4

Another part of the field. Alarum. Enter Brutus,
Messala, Young Cato, Lucilius, *and* Flavius, Labeo

Brutus

1 *yet . . . heads*: still be courageous.

Yet, countrymen, O, yet hold up your heads!
                    [*Exit with* Messala, Flavius, *and* Labeo
Cato

2 *What . . . not*: Every true-born Roman
will fight bravely.

4 *Marcus Cato*: See *2*, 1, 295 note.

What bastard doth not? Who will go with me?
I will proclaim my name about the field.
I am the son of Marcus Cato, ho!
5 A foe to tyrants, and my country's friend.
I am the son of Marcus Cato, ho!

Enter Soldiers *and fight*

Lucilius
And I am Brutus, Marcus Brutus, I,
Brutus, my country's friend. Know me for Brutus!

Young Cato is slain

O young and noble Cato, art thou down?
10 Why, now thou diest as bravely as Titinius
And mayst be honour'd, being Cato's son.
First Soldier
Yield, or thou diest.
Lucilius
                    Only I yield to die.

12 *Only I yield*: I yield only.
13 *straight*: immediately.

There is so much that thou wilt kill me straight.

Giving him money

14 *in his death*: for killing him.

Kill Brutus and be honour'd in his death.
First Soldier
15 We must not. A noble prisoner!

Enter Antony

16 *Room ho*: make way.

Second Soldier
Room ho! Tell Antony, Brutus is ta'en.
First Soldier
I'll tell the news. Here comes the general.
Brutus is ta'en, Brutus is ta'en, my lord!
Antony
Where is he?
Lucilius
20 Safe, Antony, Brutus is safe enough.
I dare assure thee that no enemy
Shall ever take alive the noble Brutus.
The gods defend him from so great a shame!
24 *or . . . or*: either . . . or.
25 *like himself*: true to his own nature.
When you do find him, or alive or dead,
25 He will be found like Brutus, like himself.
Antony
This is not Brutus, friend, but, I assure you,
A prize no less in worth. Keep this man safe,
Give him all kindness. I had rather have
Such men my friends than enemies. Go on,
30 *whe'er*: whether.
30 And see whe'er Brutus be alive or dead,
And bring us word unto Octavius' tent
32 *is chanc'd*: has turned out.
How everything is chanc'd. [*Exeunt*

Act 5 Scene 5
The rebels are defeated and Brutus kills
himself. Antony speaks his obituary.

SCENE 5

Another part of the field. Enter Brutus, Dardanius,
Clitus, Strato, *and* Volumnius

1 *remains*: survivors.

Brutus
Come, poor remains of friends, rest on this rock.
Clitus
2 *Statilius . . . light*: This should have
been a signal that all was well in
another part of the battlefield.
3 *or . . . or*: either . . . or.
4 *the word*: the right word.
5 *in fashion*: that is popular now.
Statilius show'd the torchlight but, my lord,
He came not back. He is or ta'en or slain.
Brutus
Sit thee down, Clitus. Slaying is the word,
5 It is a deed in fashion. Hark thee, Clitus. [*Whispering*]
Clitus
What, I, my lord? No, not for all the world.

Brutus
Peace then, no words.
    Clitus
                    I'll rather kill myself.
    Brutus
Hark thee, Dardanius. [*Whispers*]
    Dardanius
                  Shall I do such a deed?
    Clitus
O Dardanius!
    Dardanius

10 O Clitus!
    Clitus

11 *ill*: bad.

What ill request did Brutus make to thee?
    Dardanius
To kill him, Clitus. Look, he meditates.
    Clitus

13 *vessel*: body, person.

Now is that noble vessel full of grief,

14 *it . . . eyes*: his eyes are overflowing
with tears.

That it runs over even at his eyes.
    Brutus

15 *list*: listen.

15 Come hither, good Volumnius, list a word.
    Volumnius
What says my lord?
    Brutus
              Why, this, Volumnius:
The ghost of Caesar hath appear'd to me

18 *several*: separate.

Two several times by night, at Sardis once
And this last night here in Philippi fields.

20 *hour*: time to die.

20 I know my hour is come.
    Volumnius
               Not so, my lord.
    Brutus
Nay, I am sure it is, Volumnius.

22 *the world . . . goes*: how things have
turned out.
23 *pit*: hole in which hunted animals are
trapped; grave.

Thou seest the world, Volumnius, how it goes:
Our enemies have beat us to the pit.

Low alarums

24 *worthy*: honourable.

It is more worthy to leap in ourselves

25 *tarry*: wait.

25 Than tarry till they push us. Good Volumnius,
Thou know'st that we two went to school together;

27 *Even . . . love*: for the sake of that old friendship.

28 *sword-hilts*: sword-handle.

Even for that our love of old, I prithee
Hold thou my sword-hilts whilst I run on it.
    Volumnius
That's not an office for a friend, my lord.

Alarum still

Clitus
30 Fly, fly, my lord, there is no tarrying here.
    Brutus
Farewell to you, and you, and you, Volumnius.
Strato, thou hast been all this while asleep:
Farewell to thee too, Strato. Countrymen,
My heart doth joy that yet in all my life

36 *this losing day*: today's defeat.

35 I found no man but he was true to me.
I shall have glory by this losing day
More than Octavius and Mark Antony

38 *vile*: dishonourable.

By this vile conquest shall attain unto.

39 *at once*: all together; once and for all.

So fare you well at once, for Brutus' tongue

40 *his*: its.

40 Hath almost ended his life's history.

41–2 *Night . . . hour*: my eyes are heavy with sleep, and my body needs rest, having fought on only to achieve this hour (of death).

Night hangs upon mine eyes, my bones would rest,
That have but labour'd to attain this hour.

Alarum. Cry within, 'Fly, fly, fly!'

Clitus
Fly, my lord, fly!
Brutus
                  Hence! I will follow.
       [*Exeunt* Clitus, Dardanius, *and* Volumnius
I prithee, Strato, stay thou by thy lord.

45 *respect*: reputation.

45 Thou art a fellow of a good respect,

46 *smatch*: touch.

Thy life hath had some smatch of honour in it.
Hold then my sword and turn away thy face,
While I do run upon it. Wilt thou, Strato?
    Strato
Give me your hand first. Fare you well, my lord.
    Brutus
50 Farewell, good Strato.

Runs on his sword

Caesar, now be still,

I kill'd not thee with half so good a will.   [*Dies*

Alarum. Retreat. Enter Antony, Octavius, Messala,
Lucilius, *and the army*

Octavius
What man is that?
Messala
My master's man. Strato, where is thy master?
Strato
Free from the bondage you are in, Messala.
55 The conquerors can but make a fire of him:
For Brutus only overcame himself,
And no man else hath honour by his death.
Lucilius
So Brutus should be found. I thank thee, Brutus,
That thou hast prov'd Lucilius' saying true.
Octavius
60 All that serv'd Brutus I will entertain them.
Fellow, wilt thou bestow thy time with me?
Strato
Ay, if Messala will prefer me to you.
Octavius
Do so, good Messala.
Messala
How died my master, Strato?
Strato
65 I held the sword, and he did run on it.
Messala
Octavius, then take him to follow thee,
That did the latest service to my master.
Antony
This was the noblest Roman of them all:
All the conspirators, save only he,
70 Did that they did in envy of great Caesar.
He only, in a general honest thought
And common good to all, made one of them.
His life was gentle, and the elements
So mix'd in him that Nature might stand up
75 And say to all the world, 'This was a man!'

51 *with . . . will*: half as willingly.

51s.d. *Retreat*: The trumpet signal to recall soldiers pursuing the enemy.

55 *make . . . him*: burn his body on a funeral pyre.
56 *only*: alone.

59 *Lucilius' saying*: See *5, 4, 21–2*.

60 *entertain them*: take them into my service.
61 *bestow*: spend.

62 *prefer*: recommend.

67 *latest*: last.
69 *save*: except.
71–2 *He only . . . them*: he joined the conspirators only because he honestly believed that this was for the general good of all the people; see 'Shakespeare's Plutarch', p.110.
73 *gentle*: noble.
73–4 *the elements . . . man*: Elizabethan physiology taught that there were four elements (earth, water, fire, air), present in the human body, and that their combination would determine the individual personality; the mixture in Brutus produced the perfect man.

76 *According . . . him*: let us treat him
    with the honour he deserves.
    virtue: inherent worth; the Latin *virtùs*
    encompassed masculine (especially
    military) excellence, fortitude,
    discipline, and self-restraint.
79 *Most . . . soldier*: with full military
    honours.
    order'd: treated.
80 *field*: army.
81 *part*: share.

Octavius
According to his virtue let us use him,
With all respect and rites of burial.
Within my tent his bones tonight shall lie,
Most like a soldier, order'd honourably.
80 So call the field to rest, and let's away
To part the glories of this happy day.   [*Exeunt*

'This was the noblest Roman of them all.' (*5*, 5, 68). David Schofield as Mark
Antony, Royal Shakespeare Company, 1984.

Shakespeare's Plutarch

The following passages are taken from Sir Thomas North's translation (1579) of Plutarch's *Lives of the Greeks and Romans.*[1]

Act 1, Scene 2

lines 1–9
At that time the feast *Lupercalia* was celebrated . . . that day there are divers noblemen's sons, young men . . . which run naked through the city, striking in sport them they meet in their way with leather thongs . . . And many noblewomen and gentlewomen also go of purpose to stand in their way, and do put forth their hands to be stricken . . . persuading themselves that, being with child, they shall have good delivery, and also, being barren, that it will make them to conceive with child. (page 82)

lines 3–7,
234–49
Antonius . . . was one of them that ran this holy course. So, when he came into the market-place, the people made a lane for him to run at liberty; and he came to Caesar and presented him a diadem wreathed about with laurel. Whereupon there rose a cry of rejoicing, not very great, done only by a few appointed for the purpose. But when Caesar refused the diadem, then all the people together made an outcry of joy. Then Antonius offering it him again, there was a second shout of joy, but yet of a few. But when Caesar refused it again the second time, then all the whole people shouted. Caesar having made this proof found that the people did not like of it, and thereupon rose out of his chair, and commanded the crown to be carried unto Jupiter in the Capitol. (page 83)

lines 192–5
Caesar also had Cassius in great jealousy and suspected him much. Whereupon he said on a time to his friends: 'What will Cassius do, think ye? I like not his pale looks.' Another time when Caesar's friends complained unto him . . . he answered them again 'As for those fat men and smooth-combed heads', quoth he, 'I never reckon of them. But these pale-visaged and carrion lean people, I fear them most.'— meaning Brutus and Cassius. (page 85)

[1] *Shakespeare's Plutarch*, ed. T. J. B. Spencer (Penguin, 1964). All page references are taken from this edition.

Act 2, Scene 3 *and* **Act 3, Scene 1**, lines 3–12

And one Artemidorus . . . [who] was very familiar with certain of Brutus' confederates and therefore knew the most part of all their practices against Caesar, came and brought him a little bill written with his own hand . . . Caesar took it of him, but could never read it, for the number of people that did salute him.   (page 91)

Act 3, Scene 1

lines 27–76   So, Caesar coming into the [Senate] house, all the Senate stood up on their feet to do him honour. Then part of Brutus' company and confederates stood round about Caesar's chair, and part of them also came towards him, as though they made suit with Metellus Cimber, to call home his brother again from banishment; and thus, prosecuting still their suit, they followed Caesar till he was set in his chair; who denying their petitions and being offended with them one after another, because the more they were denied, the more they pressed upon him and were the earnester with him. Metellus at length, taking his gown with both his hands, pulled it over his neck, which was the sign given the confederates to set upon him.   (pages 92–3)

Then Casca behind strake him in the neck with his sword. Howbeit the wound was not great nor mortal, because, it seemed, the fear of such a devilish attempt did amaze him and take his strength from him, that he killed him not on the first blow.   (page 93)

They on the other side that had conspired his death compassed him in on every side with their swords drawn in their hands, that Caesar turned him nowhere but he was stricken at by some, and still had naked swords in his face, and was hacked and mangled among them, as a wild beast taken of hunters. For it was agreed among them that every man should give him a wound, because all their parts should be in this murder.   (page 94)

line 77   Men report also that Caesar did still defend himself against the rest, running every way with his body. But when he saw Brutus with his sword drawn in his hand, then he pulled his gown over his head and made no more resistance, and was driven, either casually or purposedly by the counsel of the conspirators, against the base whereon Pompey's image stood, which ran all of a gore-blood till he was slain.

(pages 94–5)

lines 78–121   Brutus and his consorts, having their swords bloody in their hands, went straight to the Capitol, persuading the Romans, as they went, to take their liberty again. Now at the first time, when the murder was newly done, there were sudden outcries of people that ran up and down the city; the which indeed did the more increase the fear and tumult . . . Brutus made an oration unto them to win the favour of the people and to justify what they had done. All those that were by said they had done well, and cried unto them that they should boldly come down from the Capitol. Whereupon, Brutus and his companions came boldly down into the market-place. The rest followed in troop; but Brutus went foremost, very honourably compassed in round about with the noblest men of the city, which brought him from the Capitol, through the market-place, to the pulpit for orations.   (pages 125–6)

lines 227–51   Then Antonius thinking good his testament should be read openly, and also that his body should be honourably buried and not in hugger-mugger, lest the people might thereby take occasion to be worse offended if they did otherwise, Cassius stoutly spake against it. But Brutus went with the motion, and agreed unto it. Wherein it seemeth he committed a second fault. For the first fault he did was when he would not consent to his fellow conspirators that Antonius should be slain; and therefore he was justly accused that thereby he had saved and strengthened a strong and grievous enemy of their conspiracy. The second fault was when he agreed that Caesar's funerals should be as Antonius would have them; the which indeed marred all.

    (pages 127–8)

Act 3, Scene 2

lines 73–266   Afterwards, when Caesar's body was brought into the market-place, Antonius making his funeral oration in praise of the dead, according to the ancient custom of Rome, and perceiving that his words moved the common people to compassion, he framed his eloquence to make their hearts yearn the more; and, taking Caesar's gown all bloody in his hand, he laid it open to the sight of them all, showing what a number of cuts and holes it had upon it. Therewithal the people fell presently into such a rage and mutiny that there was no more order kept amongst the common people. For some of them cried out: 'Kill the murderers'. Others plucked up forms, tables and stalls about the market-place . . . and having laid them all on a heap together, they set them on fire, and thereupon did put the body of Caesar, and burnt it in the middest of the most holy places. And furthermore, when the fire was throughly kindled, some here, some there, took burning fire-brands, and ran **with** them to the murderers' houses that had killed him, to set them **a-fire.** Howbeit the conspirators, foreseeing the danger before, had **wisely** provided for themselves, and fled.   (pages 128–9)

Act 3, Scene 3

But there was a poet called Cinna, who had been no partaker **of the** conspiracy but was alway one of Caesar's chiefest friends . . . when **he** heard that they carried Caesar's body to burial, being ashamed **not to** accompany his funerals, he went out of his house, and thrust **himself** into the press of the common people that were in a great uproar. **And** because some one called him by his name, Cinna, the people **thinking** he had been that Cinna who in an oration he had made had spoken **very** evil of Caesar, they falling upon him in their rage slew him outright **in** the market-place.   (pages 129–30)

Act 4, Scene 2 *and* 3

lines 1–52,
1–138

About that time Brutus sent to pray Cassius to come to the city **of** Sardis; and so he did . . . Now as it commonly happeneth in great **affairs** between two persons, both of them having many friends and so **many** captains under them, there ran tales and complaints betwixt **them.** Therefore . . . they went into a little chamber together, and bade **every** man avoid, and did shut the doors to them. Then they began to **pour** out their complaints one to another, and grew hot and loud, **earnestly** accusing one another, and at length fell both a-weeping . . . [Eventually Marcus Faonius] in despite of the doorkeepers, came into the **chamber,** and, with a certain scoffing and mocking gesture which **he** counterfeited of purpose, he rehearsed the verses which old Nestor **said** in Homer:

> My lords, I pray you hearken both to me,
> For I have seen moe years than suchie three.

Cassius fell a-laughing at him. But Brutus thrust him out of **the** chamber, and called him dog and counterfeit Cynic. Howbeit **his** coming in brake their strife at that time; and so they left each other.
                    (pages 145–6)

lines 275–86

But, above all, the ghost that appeared unto Brutus showed plainly **that** the gods were offended with the murder of Caesar. The vision was **thus.** Brutus . . . slept every night, as his manner was, in his tent; and being **yet** awake thinking of his affairs—for by report he was as careful a **captain** and lived with as little sleep as ever man did—he thought he heard a noise at his tent door; and, looking towards the light of the lamp that waxed very dim, he saw a horrible vision of a man, of a wonderful greatness and dreadful look, which at the first made him marvellously afraid. But when he saw that it did him no hurt, but stood by his bedside and said nothing, at length he asked him what he was. The image answered him: 'I am thy ill angel, Brutus, and thou shalt see me by the city of Philippes.' Then Brutus replied again, and said: 'Well, I shall see thee then.' Therewithal the spirit presently vanished from him.

(pages 99–100)

Act 5, Scene 1

lines 93–118 [Cassius said] 'The gods grant us, O Brutus, that this day we may win the field and ever after to live all the rest of our life quietly one with another. But sith the gods have so ordained it that the greatest and chiefest things amongst men are most uncertain, and that, if the battle fall out otherwise today than we wish or look for, we shall hardly meet again, what art thou then determined to do—to fly, or die?' Brutus answered him:

> 'Being yet a young man and not over greatly experienced in the world, I trust (I know not how) a certain rule of philosophy by the which I did greatly blame and reprove Cato for killing of himself, as being no lawful nor godly act, touching the gods, nor, concerning men, valiant; not to give place and yield to divine providence, and not constantly and patiently to take whatsoever it pleaseth him to send us, but to draw back and fly. But being now in the midst of the danger, I am of a contrary mind. For, if it be not the will of God that this battle fall out fortunate for us, I will look no more for hope, neither seek to make any new supply for war again, but will rid me of this miserable world, and content me with my fortune. For I gave up my life for my country in the Ides of March, for the which I shall live in another more glorious world.' (pages 154–5)

Act 5, Scene 5

lines 1–51 Now, the night being far spent, Brutus as he sat bowed towards Clitus one of his men and told him somewhat in his ear, the other answered him not, but fell a-weeping. Thereupon he proved Dardanus, and said somewhat also to him. At length he came to Volumnius himself, and, speaking to him in Greek, prayed him, for the study's sake which brought them acquainted together, that he would help him to put his hand to his sword, to thrust it in him to kill him. Volumnius denied his request, and so did many others. And, amongst the rest, one of them said, there was no tarrying for them there, but that they must needs fly. Then Brutus rising up:

> 'We must fly indeed,' he said, 'but it must be with our hands not with our feet.'

Then, taking every man by the hand, he said these words unto them with a cheerful countenance:

> 'It rejoiceth my heart that not one of my friends hath failed me at my need, and I do not complain of my fortune, but only for my country's sake. For, as for me, I think myself happier than they that have overcome, considering that I leave a perpetual fame of our courage and manhood, the which our enemies the conquerors shall never attain unto by force nor money, neither can let their posterity to say that they, being naughty and unjust men, have slain good men, to usurp tyrannical power not pertaining to them.'

Having said so, he prayed every man to shift for themselves. And then he went a little aside with two or three only, among the which Strato was one . . . He came as near to him as he could, and, taking his sword by the hilts with both his hands and falling down upon the point of it, ran himself through. Others say that not he, but Strato, at his request, held the sword in his hand, and turned his head aside, and that Brutus fell down upon it; and so ran himself through, and died presently.

(pages 170–2)

lines 68–75   Antonius spake it openly divers times that he thought that of all them that had slain Caesar there was none but Brutus only that was moved to do it as thinking the act commendable of itself; but that all the other conspirators did conspire his death for some private malice or envy that they otherwise did bear unto him.   (page 140)

Classwork and Examinations

The plays of Shakespeare are studied all over the world, and this classroom edition is being used in many different countries. Teaching methods vary from school to school—even *within* the United Kingdom—and there are many different ways of examining a student's work. Some teachers and examiners expect detailed knowledge of Shakespeare's text; others ask for imaginative involvement with his characters and their situations; and there are some teachers who want their students, by means of 'workshop' activities, to share in the theatrical experience of directing and performing a play. Most people use a variety of methods. This section of the book offers a few suggestions for approaches to *Julius Caesar* which could be used in schools and colleges to help with students' understanding and *enjoyment* of the play.

  A Discussion of Themes and Topics
  B Character Study
  C Activities
  D Context Questions
  E Critical Appreciation
  F Essays
  G Projects

A Discussion of Themes and Topics

It is most sensible to discuss each scene as it is read, sharing impressions (and perhaps correcting misapprehensions): no two people experience any character in quite the same way, and we all have different expectations. It can be useful to compare aspects of this play with other fictions—plays, novels, films—or with modern life. A large class can divide into small groups, each with a leader, who can discuss different aspects of a single topic and then report back to the main assembly.

Suggestions

A1 Do you think the two tribunes, Flavius and Murellus, are just spoil-sports?

A2 Cassius seems to think that past medical history, and a known physical disability ('the falling sickness'—i.e. epilepsy), make Caesar unfit for a position of power. Should such things be taken into consideration when a person is considered for a job?

A3   Caesar objects that Cassius has no cultural interests in his life: 'he loves no plays . . . he hears no music'. Do you think that these things are important?

A4   Brutus feels he must choose between love of his friend and love of his country; can you imagine having to make a comparable choice in your own life?

A5   Cassius suggests that the people get the government they deserve: Caesar 'would not be a wolf But that he sees the Romans are but sheep' (1, 3, 104–5). How far do you agree with his view?

A6   Brutus looks to the past to find a precedent for his actions:

> My ancestors did from the streets of Rome
> The Tarquin drive when he was call'd a king.   (2, 1, 53–4)

Is this a sensible thing to do? What sort of lessons can we learn from history?

A7   Portia reproaches Brutus for his secrecy:

> You have some sick offence within your mind,
> Which, by the right and virtue of my place
> I ought to know of   (2, 1, 268–70).

Should husbands and wives ever keep secrets from each other?

A8   Before he goes to the Capitol, Caesar consults the 'augurers' (*Act 2*, Scene 2). Do you read your horoscope—and if so, do you take any notice of it?

A9   Do you think that dreams have any importance?

A10 Portia, Brutus, and Cassius all take their own lives. Are their suicides heroic—or are they all the acts of cowards?

B   Character Study   Shakespeare's characters can be studied in many different ways, either from the *outside*, where the detached, critical student (or group of students) can see the function of every character within the whole scheme and pattern of the play; or from the *inside*, where the sympathetic student (like an actor) can identify with a single character and can look at the action and the other characters from his/her point of view.

Suggestions   a) from 'outside' the characters

B1   Describe the character of Casca. Why does Shakespeare use a character like this to narrate the action on the feast of Lupercal (1, 2, 220–85)?

B2   If you were directing a production of the play, would you omit the character of Cicero? What is his function?

B3   Make a detailed character-study of Caesar *as he appears in this play*. Do you think that Shakespeare is showing us the whole man?

B4   Why is Lucius important to the play?

B5   Can you ever think of the conspirators as 'The men that gave their country liberty' (3, 1, 118)?

b) from 'inside' a character

B6   Imagine you are one of the Citizens who 'vanish tongue-tied' when they are scolded by the tribunes in *Act 1*, Scene 1. Describe your feelings.

B7   Brutus *says* very little when Cassius is talking about Caesar in *Act 1*, Scene 2; but what is he *thinking*? In the character of Brutus, write a stream-of-consciousness account of the thoughts passing through your mind at this time, *or*, write your diary entry for this day.

B8   Casca is a very 'biased' reporter of the proceedings on the feast of Lupercal (1, 2, 220–285). How would the event be described by an impartial observer, *or* by a loyal supporter of Caesar?

B9   As one of the conspirators, or else a close personal friend, give a description of Cassius as you knew him before the murder of Julius Caesar.

B10   You are the boy Lucius. What can you remember of the night before the ides of March?

B11   Some of the Citizens choose to listen to Cassius rather than Brutus (3, 2, 9). What sort of speech would Cassius make?

B12   In the character of Brutus, write a letter to Portia before you make your escape from Rome, explaining your part in the conspiracy. Why are you leaving her now?

B13   The poet Cinna would have written an elegy to be read at Caesar's funeral. Write such a poem.

B14 After the death of Cassius, Pindarus determines to escape 'Far from this country' (5, 3, 49). Living among strangers, how will he tell them of the things he has witnessed and the master he has served?

C   Activities   These can involve two or more students, preferably working *away from* the desk or study-table and using gesture and position ('body-language') as well as speech. They can help students to develop a sense of drama and the dramatic aspects of Shakespeare's play—which was written to be *performed*, not studied in a classroom.

Suggestions   **C1**   Speak the lines—act the scenes! To familiarize yourselves with Shakespeare's verse, try different reading techniques—reading by punctuation marks (where each person hands over to the next at every punctuation mark); reading by sentences; and reading by speeches. Begin acting with small units—about ten lines—where two or three characters are speaking to each other; rehearse these in groups of students, and perform them before the whole class. Read the lines from a script—then act them out in your own words.

C2   You are radio or television reporters sent to cover the sporting events in Rome at the feast of Lupercal. Give running commentaries—perhaps signed for deaf people—on the action.

C3   Reporters from all the media are sent to the formal ceremonies at the Capitol (as to the opening of Parliament) on the ides of March—but events take a surprising turn! Capture all the excitement for your viewers/listeners/readers.

C4   Portia sends Lucius to the Capitol to see Brutus, and tells him 'Come to me again And bring me word what he doth say' (2, 4, 45–6). Devise a scene where Lucius returns home, and tells his mistress what has happened.

C5   Deliver the orations of Brutus and Antony (*Act* 3, Scene 2), and have them fully reported in newspapers of varying quality, and on television or radio with 'voice-over' translations into modern English (or any other language with which you are familiar). Can you arrange for them to be signed for deaf people?

C6   There are two passages relating to the death of Portia (4, 3, 144–158, *and* 181–195). By performing these two excerpts, try to decide whether they are mutually exclusive, or whether they could complement each other. If one must go, which would you—as director and actors—prefer to retain?

D Context Questions

Questions like these, which are sometimes used in written examinations, can also be helpful as a class revision quiz, testing knowledge of the play and some understanding of its words.

D1   She dreamt tonight she saw my statue,
Which like a fountain with an hundred spouts
Did run pure blood, and many lusty Romans
Came smiling and did bathe their hands in it.
And these does she apply for warnings and portents
And evils imminent.

    (i)   Who is speaking, and to whom does he speak?
    (ii)   How exactly does the dreamer interpret the dream? What does she want the speaker to do?
    (iii)   How does the listener interpret the dream?
    (iv)   Which is the correct interpretation?

D2   Thou seest the world, Volumnius, how it goes:
Our enemies have beat us to the pit.
It is more worthy to leap in ourselves
Than tarry till they push us.

    (i)   Who is the speaker?
    (ii)   What is the occasion?
    (iii)   What does the speaker ask Volumnius to do, and what does Volumnius reply?
    (iv)   What is the speaker's reaction to Volumnius's reply?

D3   The skies are painted with unnumber'd sparks,
They are all fire, and every one doth shine;
But there's but one in all doth hold his place.
So in the world: 'tis furnish'd well with men,
And men are flesh and blood, and apprehensive;
Yet in the number do I know but one
That unassailable holds on his rank.

    (i)   Who is speaking, and of whom does he speak?
    (ii)   What has he been asked to do?
    (iii)   Does he consent?
    (iv)   What happens next?

D4   For this present,
I would not (so with love I might entreat you)
Be any further mov'd. What you have said
I will consider; what you have to say

I will with patience hear and find a time
Both meet to hear and answer such high things.

(i)   Who is speaking, and to whom does he speak?
(ii)   What is the occasion?
(iii)   What are the 'high things' that have been discussed?
(iv)   How does the speaker eventually answer them?

D5   There is my dagger
And here my naked breast: within, a heart
Dearer than Pluto's mine, richer than gold.
If that thou beest a Roman, take it forth,
I that denied thee gold will give my heart:
Strike as thou didst at Caesar.

(i)   Who is speaking, and where is the scene?
(ii)   What has the speaker been accused of?
(iii)   By whom has he been accused?
(iv)   What is the real cause of the accuser's distress?

D6   Is it excepted I should know no secrets
That appertain to you? Am I your self
But, as it were, in sort or limitation,
To keep with you at meals, comfort your bed,
And talk to you sometimes?

(i)   Who is speaking, and to whom?
(ii)   What secret does the speaker want to know?
(iii)   What has the speaker just done, and why?
(iv)   What happens to the speaker at the end of the play?

E   Critical Appreciation   Some examination boards allow candidates to take their copies of the play into the examination room, asking them to re-read specified sections of the play (such as the one printed here) and answer questions on them.

E1   *Act 1*, Scene 2, lines 115–41
Cassius
                              And this man   115
Is now become a god, and Cassius is
A wretched creature and must bend his body
If Caesar carelessly but nod on him.
He had a fever when he was in Spain,
And when the fit was on him I did mark   120

How he did shake. 'Tis true, this god did shake,
His coward lips did from their colour fly,
And that same eye whose bend doth awe the world
Did lose his lustre. I did hear him groan,
Ay, and that tongue of his that bade the Romans   125
Mark him and write his speeches in their books,
'Alas', it cried, 'give me some drink, Titinius',
As a sick girl. Ye gods, it doth amaze me
A man of such a feeble temper should
So get the start of the majestic world   130
And bear the palm alone.

Shout. Flourish

Brutus
Another general shout!
I do believe that these applauses are
For some new honours that are heap'd on Caesar.
   Cassius
Why, man, he doth bestride the narrow world   135
Like a Colossus, and we petty men
Walk under his huge legs and peep about
To find ourselves dishonourable graves.
Men at some time are masters of their fates:
The fault, dear Brutus, is not in our stars   140
But in ourselves, that we are underlings.

What does this description tell you about Julius Caesar? What can you learn from it about the character of Cassius? Comment on the placing of the stage direction '*Shout. Flourish*'.

E2   Read again *Act 2*, Scene 1, lines 1–34 (from '*Enter* Brutus *in his orchard*' to 'kill him in the shell'). What do you learn from this passage about the character of Brutus? Do you find his arguments convincing? How important is the presence of Lucius in this episode?

E3   Re-read *Act 3*, Scene 1, lines 121s.d.–163 (from '*Enter a* Servant' to 'The choice and master spirits of this age'). Comment on Antony's diplomatic treatment of Caesar's murderers, or use this passage for a discussion of Shakespeare's use of Servants in this play.

F   Essays   These will usually give you a specific topic to discuss, or perhaps a question that must be answered, in writing, *with a reasoned argument*.

They *never* want you to tell the story of the play—so don't! Your examiner—or teacher—has read the play and does not need to be reminded of it. Relevant quotations will always help you to make your points more strongly.

F1 Describe the character of Cassius, showing how our attitude to him changes towards the end of the play.

F2 On three occasions Brutus refuses to listen to advice from Cassius; say what these occasions are, and explain Brutus's reasons for not taking the advice.

F3 What contributions to the play are made by Calpurnia and Portia?

F4 Is Mark Antony a loyal friend to Caesar, or a skilful politician working for his own ends?

F5 Give an account of the part played in *Julius Caesar* by the Roman citizens.

F6 How important is the supernatural in *Julius Caesar*?

F7 How does Shakespeare maintain our interest in the play once its hero, Julius Caesar, is dead?

F8 Why do Brutus and Cassius lose the battle at Philippi?

F9 Describe some of the different effects achieved by Shakespeare's use of prose in *Julius Caesar*.

F10 'In *Julius Caesar* there are no moral absolutes: no character is entirely good or entirely bad'. Do you agree?

F11 At the beginning of the play, Brutus declares that Antony 'is but a limb of Caesar' (2, 1, 165). Show how Shakespeare develops the character of Mark Antony as the play progresses.

G Projects In some schools students are asked to do more 'free-ranging' work, which takes them outside the text—but which should always be relevant to the play. Such Projects may demand skills other than reading and writing: design and artwork, for instance, may be involved. Sometimes a 'portfolio' of work is assembled over a considerable period of time; and this can be presented to the examiner as part of the student's work for assessment.

The availability of resources will, obviously, do much to determine the nature of the Projects; but this is something that only the local teachers will understand. However, there is always help to be found in libraries, museums, and art galleries.

G1 In the modern world, the death of a public figure is given great 'media coverage'. Present the assassination of Julius Caesar in this way.

G2 Julius Caesar's contribution to civilization.

G3 Revolutions.

G4 Foretelling the future.

G5 Dreams and their significance.

G6 The wives of great men.

G7 Horoscopes.

G8 Make a study of political assassinations, comparing the plot against Caesar with (for example) the murder of John F. Kennedy in 1963, or the attempted Russian 'coup' in August 1991.

Background

England c. *1599*

When Shakespeare was writing *Julius Caesar*, most people believed that the sun went round the earth. They were taught that this was a divinely ordered scheme of things, and that—in England—God had instituted a Church and ordained a Monarchy for the right government of the land and the populace.

'The past is a foreign country; they do things differently there.'

L. P. Hartley

Government For most of Shakespeare's life, the reigning monarch was Elizabeth I. With her counsellors and ministers she governed the nation (population five million) from London, although fewer than half a million people inhabited the capital city. In the rest of the country, law and order were maintained by the land-owners and enforced by their deputies. The average man had no vote—and his wife had no rights at all.

Religion At this time, England was a Christian country. All children were baptized, soon after they were born, into the Church of England; they were taught the essentials of the Christian faith, and instructed in their duty to God and to humankind.

Marriages were performed, and funerals conducted, only by the licensed clergy and in accordance with the Church's rites and ceremonies. Attendance at divine service was compulsory; absences (without good—medical—reason) could be punished by fines. By such means, the authorities were able to keep some check on the populace—recording births, marriages, and deaths; being alert to any religious nonconformity, which could be politically dangerous; and ensuring a minimum of orthodox instruction through the official 'Homilies' which were regularly preached from the pulpits of all parish churches throughout the realm.

Following Henry VIII's break away from the Church of Rome, all people in England were able to hear the church services *in their own language*. The Book of Common Prayer was used in every church, and an English translation of the Bible was read aloud in public. The Christian religion had never been so well taught before!

Education   School education reinforced the Church's teaching. From the age of four, boys might attend the 'petty school' (French '*petite école*') to learn the rudiments of reading and writing along with a few prayers; some schools also included work with numbers. At the age of seven, the boy was ready for the grammar school (if his father was willing and able to pay the fees). Here, a thorough grounding in Latin grammar was followed by translation work and the study of Roman authors, paying attention as much to style as to matter. The arts of fine writing were thus inculcated from early youth.

A very few students proceeded to university; these were either clever scholarship boys, or else the sons of noblemen. Girls stayed at home, and acquired domestic and social skills—cooking, sewing, perhaps even music. The lucky ones might learn to read and write.

Language   At the start of the sixteenth century the English had a very poor opinion of their own language: there was little serious writing in English, and hardly any literature. Latin was the language of international scholarship, and Englishmen admired the eloquence of the Romans. They made many translations, and in this way they extended the resources of their own language, increasing its vocabulary and stretching its grammatical structures. French, Italian, and Spanish works were also translated, and—for the first time—there were English versions of the Bible.

By the end of the century, English was a language to be proud of: it was rich in synonyms, capable of infinite variety and subtlety, and ready for all kinds of word-play—especially the *puns*, for which Shakespeare's English is renowned.

Drama   The great art-form of the Elizabethans was their drama. They inherited a tradition of play-acting from the Middle Ages, and this was reinforced in the sixteenth century by their reading and translating the Roman playwrights. At the beginning of the century, plays were performed by groups of actors, all-male companies (boys acted the female roles) who travelled from town to town, setting up their stages in open places (such as inn-yards) or, with the permission of the owner, in the hall of a noble house. The touring companies continued, in the provinces, into the seventeenth century; but in London, in 1576, a new building was erected for the performance of plays. This was the Theatre, the first purpose-built playhouse in England. Other playhouses followed (including Shakespeare's own theatre, the Globe); and the English drama reached new heights of eloquence.

There were those who disapproved, of course. The theatres, which brought large crowds together, could encourage the spread of disease— and dangerous ideas. During the summer, when the plague was at its worst, the playhouses were closed. A constant censorship was imposed, more or less severe at different times. The Puritan faction tried to close down the theatres, but—partly because there was royal favour for the drama, and partly because the buildings were outside the city limits— they did not succeed until 1642.

Theatre From contemporary comments and sketches—most particularly a drawing by a Dutch visitor, Johannes de Witt—it is possible to form some idea of the typical Elizabethan playhouse for which most of Shakespeare's plays were written. Hexagonal in shape, it had three roofed galleries encircling an open courtyard. The plain, high stage projected into the yard, where it was surrounded by the audience of standing 'groundlings'. At the back were two doors for the actors' entrances and exits, and between these doors was a curtained 'discovery space' (sometimes called an 'inner stage'). Above this was a balcony, used as a musicians' gallery or for the performance of scenes 'above', and projecting over part of the stage was a roof, supported on two pillars, which was painted with the sun, moon, and stars for the 'heavens'.

Underneath was space (concealed by curtaining) which could be used by characters ascending and descending through a trap-door in the stage. Costumes and properties were kept backstage in the 'tiring house'. The actors dressed lavishly, often wearing the secondhand clothes bestowed by rich patrons. Stage properties were important for defining a location, but the dramatist's own words were needed to explain the time of day, since all performances took place in the early afternoon.

A replica of Shakespeare's own theatre, the Globe, has been built in London, and stands in Southwark, almost exactly on the Bankside site of the original.

Shakespeare's Globe, Southwark, London, England. Photograph by Richard Kalina.

Selected Further Reading

There are useful chapters, or essays, on *Julius Caesar* in the following books:

Bayley, John, *Shakespeare and Tragedy* (1981).
Blits, Jan H., *The End of the Ancient Republic: Essays on 'Julius Caesar'* (1982).
Brooke, Nicholas, *Shakespeare's Early Tragedies* (1968).
Brower, Reuben A., *Hero and Saint: Shakespeare and the Graeco-Roman Heroic Tradition* (Oxford, 1971).
Edwards, Philip, *Shakespeare: A Writer's Progress* (Cambridge, 1986).
Granville-Barker, Harley, *Prefaces to Shakespeare: 'Julius Caesar'* (1928).
Honigmann, E. A. J., *Shakespeare: Seven Tragedies* (London, 1976).
Maxwell, J. C., 'Shakespeare's Roman Plays: 1900–1956', *Shakespeare Survey*, 10 (1957).
Meht, Dieter, *Shakespeare's Tragedies: An Introduction* (Cambridge, 1983).
Proser, Matthew N., *The Heroic Image in Five Shakespearean Tragedies* (1965).
Traversi, Derek A., *Shakespeare: The Roman Plays* (London, 1963).
Ure, Peter (ed.), *Shakespeare: 'Julius Caesar'*, Casebook Series (London, 1969).

Sources: Muir, Kenneth, *The Sources of Shakespeare's Plays* (London, 1977).

Additional background reading: Bate, Jonathan, *The Genius of Shakespeare* (Picador [Macmillan], 1997).
Blake, N. F., *Shakespeare's Language: an Introduction* (London, 1983).
Gibson, Rex, *Shakespeare's Language* (Cambridge, 1997).
Honan, Park, *Shakespeare: A Life* (Oxford, 1998).
Langley, Andrew, *Shakespeare's Theatre* (Oxford, 1999).
Thomson, Peter, *Shakespeare's Theatre* (London, 1983).

William Shakespeare, 1564–1616

Elizabeth I was Queen of England when Shakespeare was born in 1564. He was the son of a tradesman who made and sold gloves in the small town of Stratford-upon-Avon, and he was educated at the grammar school in that town. Shakespeare did not go to university when he left school, but worked, perhaps, in his father's business. When he was eighteen he married Anne Hathaway, who became the mother of his daughter, Susanna, in 1583, and of twins in 1585.

There is nothing exciting, or even unusual, in this story; and from 1585 until 1592 there are no documents that can tell us anything at all about Shakespeare. But we have learned that in 1592 he was known in London, and that he had become both an actor and a playwright.

We do not know when Shakespeare wrote his first play, and indeed we are not sure of the order in which he wrote his works. If you look on page 129 at the list of his writings and their approximate dates, you will see how he started by writing plays on subjects taken from the history of England. No doubt this was partly because he was always an intensely patriotic man—but he was also a very shrewd business-man. He could see that the theatre audiences enjoyed being shown their own history, and it was certain that he would make a profit from this kind of drama.

The plays in the next group are mainly comedies, with romantic love-stories of young people who fall in love with one another, and at the end of the play marry and live happily ever after.

At the end of the sixteenth century the happiness disappears, and Shakespeare's plays become melancholy, bitter, and tragic. This change may have been caused by some sadness in the writer's life (one of his twins died in 1596). Shakespeare, however, was not the only writer whose works at this time were very serious. The whole of England was facing a crisis. Queen Elizabeth I was growing old. She was greatly loved, and the people were sad to think she must soon die; they were also afraid, for the queen had never married, and so there was no child to succeed her.

When James I came to the throne in 1603, Shakespeare continued to write serious drama—the great tragedies and the plays based on Roman history (such as *Julius Caesar*) for which he is most famous. Finally, before he retired from the theatre, he wrote another set of comedies. These all have the same theme: they tell of happiness which is lost, and then found again.

Shakespeare returned from London to Stratford, his home town. He was rich and successful, and he owned one of the biggest houses in the town. He died in 1616.

Shakespeare also wrote two long poems, and a collection of sonnets. The sonnets describe two love-affairs, but we do not know who the lovers were. Although there are many public documents concerned with his career as a writer and a business-man, Shakespeare has hidden his personal life from us. A nineteenth-century poet, Matthew Arnold, addressed Shakespeare in a poem, and wrote 'We ask and ask—Thou smilest, and art still'.

There is not even a trustworthy portrait of the world's greatest dramatist.

Approximate order of composition of Shakespeare's works

Period	Comedies	History plays	Tragedies	Poems
I	Comedy of Errors Taming of the Shrew	Henry VI, part 1 Henry VI, part 2 Henry VI, part 3	Titus Andronicus	
1594	Two Gentlemen of Verona Love's Labour's Lost	Richard III King John		Venus and Adonis Rape of Lucrece
II	Midsummer Night's Dream Merchant of Venice	Richard II Henry IV, part 1	Romeo and Juliet	
1599	Merry Wives of Windsor Much Ado About Nothing As You Like It	Henry IV, part 2 Henry V		Sonnets
III	Twelfth Night Troilus and Cressida		Julius Caesar Hamlet	
1608	Measure for Measure All's Well That Ends Well		Othello Timon of Athens King Lear Macbeth Antony and Cleopatra Coriolanus	
IV	Pericles Cymbeline			
1613	The Winter's Tale The Tempest	Henry VIII		